THE

RULES
OF WORK

THE

RULES

OF WORK

The Unspoken Truth
About Getting Ahead in
Business

RICHARD TEMPLAR

PEARSON
Prentice
Hall

Library of Congress Publication Number: 2004116371

Publisher: Tim Moore
Acquisitions Editor: Paula Sinnott
Editorial Assistant: Richard Winkler
Marketing Manager: Martin Litkowski
International Marketing Manager: Tim Galligan
Cover Designer: Sandra Schroeder
Managing Editor: Gina Kanouse
Senior Project Editor: Kristy Hart
Copy Editor: Keith Cline
Senior Compositor: Gloria Schurick
Manufacturing Buyer: Dan Uhrig

Prentice Hall offers excellent discounts on this book when ordered in quantity for bulk purchases or special sales. For more information, please contact U.S. Corporate and Government Sales, 1-800-382-3419, corpsales@pearsontechgroup.com. For sales outside the U.S., please contact International Sales, 1-317-581-3793, international@pearsontechgroup.com.

Sixth Printing August, 2005

ISBN 0-13-185838-6

Pearson Education LTD.
Pearson Education Australia PTY, Limited.
Pearson Education Singapore, Pte. Ltd.
Pearson Education North Asia, Ltd.
Pearson Education Canada, Ltd.
Pearson Educatión de Mexico, S.A. de C.V.
Pearson Education—Japan
Pearson Education Malaysia, Pte. Ltd.

Contents

Acknowledgments

I am indebted to Rachael Stock, without whose support, encouragement and enthusiasm this book would never have happened.

Introduction

I first started formulating *The Rules of Work* many, many years ago when I was an assistant manager. There was a promotion going for the next step up—manager. There were two possible candidates, myself and Rob. On paper I had more experience, more expertise, most of the staff wanted me as their manager and I generally knew the new job better. Rob, to be honest, was useless.

I was chatting with an outside consultant the company used and asked him what he thought my chances were. "Slim," he replied. I was indignant. I explained all about my experience, my expertise, my superior abilities. "Yep," he replied, "but you don't walk like a manager." "And Rob does?" "Yep, that's about the strength of it." Needless to say he was quite right and Rob got the job. I had to work under a moron. But a moron who walked right. I studied that walk very carefully.

The consultant was spot on, there was a manager's walk. I began to notice that every employee, every job, everyone in fact, had their walk. Receptionists walked in a particular way as did the cashiers, the catering staff, the office workers, the admin, the security staff—and the managers of course. Secretly, I began to practice the walk.

Looking the Part

As I spent a lot of time watching the walk I realized that there was also a manager's style of attire, of speaking, of behavior. It wasn't enough that I was good at my job and had the experience. I had to *look* as if I was better than anyone else. It wasn't just a walk—it was an entire makeover. And gradually, as I watched, I noticed that what newspaper was read was important, as was what pen was used, how you wrote, how you talked to colleagues, what you said at meetings—everything, in fact, was being judged, evaluated, acted upon. It wasn't enough to be able to do the job. If you wanted to get on you had to be seen to be the Right Type. *The Rules of Work* is about creating that type—of course, you've got to be able to do the job in the first place. But a lot of people can do that. What makes you stand out? What makes you a suitable candidate for promotion? What makes the difference?

Act One Step Ahead

I noticed that among the managers there were some who had mastered the walk, but there were others who were practicing, unconsciously, for the next walk—the general manager's walk.

I happened at that time to be traveling around a lot between different branches and noticed that among the general managers there were some who were going to stay right where they were for a long time. But there were others already practicing for their next step ahead—the regional director's walk. And style and image.

I switched from practicing the manager's walk and leaped ahead to the general manager's walk. Three months later I was promoted from assistant manager to general manager in one swift move. I was now the moron's manager.

Walk Your Talk

Rob had the walk (*Rule 15: Develop a Style That Gets You Noticed*), but unfortunately he didn't adhere sufficiently to the rules in Part 1—he didn't know the job well enough. He looked right, sounded right, but the bottom line was—he couldn't do the job as well as he should have. I was brought in over his head because they couldn't fire him—having just promoted him it would have looked bad—and they needed someone to oversee his work so that his mistakes could be rectified quickly. Rob had reached the level of his own incompetence and stayed there for several years neither improving nor particularly getting worse—just looking good and walking right. He eventually shuffled himself off sideways into running his own business—a restaurant. This failed shortly afterward because he forgot *Rule 2: Never Stand Still* —or maybe he never actually knew it. He carried on walking like a manager instead of a restaurateur. His customers never really took to him.

By practicing the general manager's walk I got the promotion, but I also got it because I paid great attention to doing my job well. Once in this new job I was, of course, completely out of my depth. I had to quickly learn not only my new role and all its responsibilities, but also the position below, which I had not really held. I had stood in for managers but I had never been a manager—now

I was the manager's manager. I was in great danger of falling flat on my face.

Never Let Anyone Know How Hard You Work

But I was, by now, a dedicated Rules player. There was only one recourse – secret learning. I spent every spare second available – evenings, weekends, lunch breaks—studying everything I could that would help me. But I told no one—*Rule 10*.

Within a short time I had mastered enough to be able to do the job well enough. And the embryonic *Rules of Work* were born.

Have a Plan

Being a general manager was both fun and painful. It was 50 per cent more work but only 20 per cent more pay. My next step, logically, was regional director. But it didn't appeal. More work, much more work but for not that much more money. I began to study *the rules in Part 3*. Where did I want to go next? What did I want to do? I was getting bored being stuck in the office all the time and all those endless dreary meetings. And all that time spent at head office. Not for me. I wanted to have fun again. I wanted to practice the Rules. I formulated my plan.

What the company didn't have was a roving troubleshooter—a sort of general manager's general manager. I put *Rule 4: Carve Out a Niche for Yourself* into play. I suggested to the chairman that a report was needed. I never suggested that this was the job I wanted, but the agenda was obvious I suppose. I got it, of course, and became a peripatetic general manager, answerable directly only to the chairman and with a job description I wrote myself. And pay? A lot more than the regional directors were on but I practiced the rules in *Part 5: Look After Yourself*. They didn't know and I didn't let on. But I cultivated their support and friendship. I was never a threat because it was obvious I wasn't after their job. They may have wanted the money I made if they had known, but they didn't want the little niche I had carved out for myself.

And I did this without being ruthless, dishonest or unpleasant. In fact I was always diplomatic when dealing with the general managers. I treated them with courtesy and politeness, even when I had to correct them on some aspect of their job. I added the rules in *Part 4* and *Part 8*.

Knowing the People Who Count

And I quickly learned that if I wanted to know what was going on in a branch, it was best to speak to the people who really knew— the cleaners, the receptionists, the cashiers, and the drivers. It was important both to identify these people and to be on the right side of them—*Rule 86*. They supplied me with more information than anyone would have believed—and all for the price of a simple "Hello Bob, how's your daughter doing at university these days?"

The Rules of Work took shape. Over the next few years I watched them grow up, gain maturity and experience. I left the corporation and founded my own consultancy. I trained managers in *The Rules of Work* and watched them go out into the world and conquer their destiny with charm and courtesy, confidence, and authority.

But I see you have questions. How do these rules work—are they manipulative? No, you don't make anyone else do anything, it is *you* that is changing and improving.

- Do I have to become someone else? No, you may need to change your behavior a bit, but not your personality or values, you'll go on being you, but a slicker, quicker you, a more successful you.

- Are they hard to learn? No, you can learn them in a week or two—but it does take a long time to really master them. But we are learning all the time and even practicing one rule is better than none at all.

- Is it easy to spot others doing them? Yes, sometimes, but the really good Rules Player will never let you see what they are doing, they're too good for that. But once you become a Rules Player too it does become easier to see what rule people are using at any particular time.

- Will I notice benefits right away? Oh yes, you betcha, immediately.

- Do I still do them? I wouldn't even admit to doing them in the first place—I'm a Rules Player after all.

- Is it ethical to use the Rules? Yes. You aren't doing anything wrong, merely utilizing your own natural skills and talents and adapting them, using them consciously. This is a key area for understanding the Rules—consciously. Everything you do will have been decided beforehand—you'll still appear spontaneous of course, you decided that as well—but you will be a conscious manipulator of any situation rather than an unconscious victim. You will be awake and aware, living in the moment, and taking advantage of your own abilities. The bottom line is that you must be able to do your job—and do it well in the first place. The Rules are not for boasters or posers or bullshitters or charlatans or coasters. You think you work hard now? It's nothing to doing the Rules successfully—now that really does take work.

And let's face it, you love to work. You love doing your job. You have to be, to be wanting to read the Rules and to want to be moving onward and upward. What I am suggesting is that you consciously think about every area of that work and make changes to improve:

- The way you do it
- How people perceive you to be doing it

If you don't practice the Rules you will muddle along, get by, maybe find what it is you are looking for. You may already know a lot of these Rules—and be practicing them—instinctively and intuitively. Now we will do them consciously. If you do you will:

- Get promoted

- Get along better with your colleagues

- Feel better about yourself

- Enjoy your work more

- Understand your job better

- Understand your boss's point of view better

- Take more pride in both yourself and your work

- Set a good example for junior staff

- Contribute more to your company

- Be valued and respected

- Spread an aura of goodwill and cooperation around you

- Be successful if you leave to start your own business

These Rules are simple and effective, safe, and practical. They are your 100 steps to building confidence and creating a new and more powerful you. And building that new you morally and ethically. You aren't going to do anything that you wouldn't expect—and appreciate—others doing to you. These Rules enhance personal standards and elevate your individual principles. They are my gift to you. They're yours. Keep them safe, keep them secret.

PART 1

WALK YOUR TALK

This is the underlying rule that governs all the others—know your job well, do it well and be better than anyone else at doing it. It's that simple. The secret part is to make sure nobody knows how hard you have to work to do it so well. You can do all your learning in secret, in private—you just don't let on, don't let anyone know you do this—and never ever let anyone know you've read this book; it is your secret bible. The important thing is to look calm and efficient, on top of everything and totally in control. You glide through your daily work with ease and confidence. You are unflappable and unstoppable. Bottom line is, however, you must be *really* good at your basic job.

Get Your Work Noticed

It's all too easy for your work to get overlooked in the busy hurly-burly of office life. You're slaving away and it can be hard to remember that you need to put in some effort to boost your individual status and personal kudos for your work. But it's important. You have to make your mark so you stand out and your promotional potential will be realized.

The best way to do this is to step outside the normal working routine. If you have to process so many widgets each day—and so does everyone else—then processing more won't do you that much good. But if you subject a report to your boss of how *everyone* could process more widgets then you'll get noticed. The unsolicited report is a brilliant way to stand out from the crowd. It shows you're thinking on your feet and using your initiative. But it mustn't be used too often. If you submit your boss to a barrage of unsolicited reports you'll get noticed but in completely the wrong way. You have to stick to certain rules:

- Only submit a report occasionally.
- Make really sure that your report will actually work—that it will do good or provide benefits.
- Make sure your name is prominently displayed.

- Make sure the report will be seen not only by your boss, but by their boss as well.
- It doesn't have to be a report—it can be an article in the company newsletter.

Of course, the very best way to get your work noticed is to be very, very good at your job. And the best way to be good at your job is to be totally dedicated to doing the job and ignoring all the rest. There is a vast amount of politics, gossip, gamesmanship, time wasting, and socializing that goes on in the name of work. It isn't work. Keep your eye on the ball and you'll be already playing with a vast advantage over your colleagues. The Rules Player stays focused. Keep your mind on the task at hand—being very good at your job—and don't get distracted.

> "THE UNSOLICITED REPORT IS A BRILLIANT WAY TO STAND OUT FROM THE CROWD."

Never Stand Still

Most people go into work each day with only one thought—getting through to going home time. During their day they will do whatever they have to, to arrive at that magic time. You won't. You won't stand still. Having got the job it seems enough for most people that they will just do it and thus remain static. But doing the job isn't the end game for you—it is merely a means to the end. And the end for you is promotion, more money, success, moving onward and upward, amassing the contacts and experience to set out on your own, whatever it is that is on your wish list—*see Part 3*. The job, in a way, is an irrelevance.

Yes, you have to do the work. And yes, you have to do it supremely well. But your eye should already be on the next step and every activity you indulge in at work should be merely a cog in your plan to move up.

While others are thinking of their next coffee break or how to get through the afternoon without actually having to do any work, you will be busy planning and executing your next manuver. In an ideal world the Rules Player will have got their work done by lunchtime, so that they have the afternoon free; to study for the next promotion, to assess the competition among close colleagues, to write the unsolicited reports to get their work noticed, to research ways to improve the work process for everyone, to further their knowledge of company procedures and history.

> ## "IN AN IDEAL WORLD THE RULES PLAYER WILL HAVE GOT THEIR WORK DONE BY LUNCHTIME, SO THAT THEY HAVE THE AFTERNOON FREE."

If you can't get your work done by lunchtime then you will have to fit all these things into and around the work. What the competition will be doing is not doing them. But you don't stand still. Never accept that doing the job is enough. That's for the others. You will be moving right along preparing, studying, analyzing, and learning.

We talked earlier about the manager's walk; well, that's what you'll be doing, practicing the manager's walk—or whoever's walk it is you need to master. You have to see promotion—or whatever else it is you want—as a movement. You keep moving or you grow moss. You have to have movement or you grow stagnant. You have to like movement or you grow roots.

Movement requires of you that you don't sit on your backside and do nothing—don't stand still.

Volunteer Carefully

A lot of people think that if they say "yes" to everything they will get noticed, get praised and get promoted. Not true. The clever manager above them will use this "I'll do it" mentality and you will end up overworked, undervalued and abused. Before you put your hand up to volunteer for anything, think very carefully. You have to ask yourself various questions:

- Why is this person asking for volunteers?
- How will this further my plan?
- How will I look to senior management if I volunteer?
- How will I look if I don't volunteer?
- Is this a dirty job that no one else wants?
- Or is this person genuinely, desperately overburdened and really in need of my help?

It might well be a dirty job that no one else wants and by volunteering you might look very good in the eyes of senior management—they think you capable of rising to a challenge, being useful and being prepared to get your sleeves rolled up and stuck in. On the other hand they might think you're a sucker. Or if you volunteer to do the filing they'll see you as a mere filing clerk. Or you might generate a load of goodwill for helping out someone in real need of support. Be careful and choose your moments. There's no point sticking your hand up if it means you're going to be seen as a monkey. Only step that one step forward when you are confident you will look good, gain benefit, or make a difference to someone who needs help.

Also be aware that sometimes you seem to have volunteered without putting your hand up or stepping forward. It just happens that sometimes all your colleagues take a collective step backward leaving you there out in the open seemingly volunteering when you really had no intention of doing so. The first time this happens you will have to ride with it and do the job—but make sure it doesn't happen again, not to a Rules Player, not twice. Keep your ear better attuned next time and feel out the collective approach and make sure you're stepping backward with the rest of them.

> "BEFORE YOU PUT YOUR HAND UP TO VOLUNTEER FOR ANYTHING, THINK VERY CAREFULLY."

Carve Out a Niche For Yourself

I once worked with a colleague who made it a great personal skill to find out stuff about customers that we couldn't. It seemed he always knew the names of their children, where they went on vacation, their birthdays—and their spouses—their favorite music and restaurants, and consequently if you had to deal with a particular customer you went to Mike and asked, politely and humbly, if he could give you some little titbit that would get you well in with the customer. Mike had carved out a niche for himself. No one asked him to become a walking encyclopedia of customer likes and dislikes. It wasn't part of his job description. It took a lot of work and unseen effort. And it was a very valuable asset. It didn't take long for the Regional Director to hear of this extra effort Mike had put in and his rise up the corporate ladder was swift, meteoric, unprecedented. That's all it took. I say "all," it was in fact a lot of work and immensely clever.

Carving out a niche means spotting a useful area that no one else has spotted. It might be as simple as being great at spreadsheets or report writing. It might be, like Mike, knowing something no one else does. It might be being brilliant with

> ## "IF THE OTHER BOSSES THINK YOU ARE A GOOD IDEA THEN YOUR BOSS REALLY HAS TO GO ALONG WITH IT."

scheduling or budgets or understanding the system. Make sure you don't make yourself indispensable or this rule backfires.

Carving out a niche for yourself often takes you out of the normal range of office activities. You get to move around more, be out of the office more often without having to explain to anyone where you are or what you are doing. This makes you stand out from the herd, gives you independence and a superior quality. I once volunteered to edit the company newsletter—bearing in mind the previous rule—and could wander about between our seven branches at will. Obviously, I always made sure my work was done on time and supremely well.

Carving out a niche for yourself frequently means you get noticed by people other than your boss—other people's bosses. These bosses get together and they talk. If they bring your name up it will be in a good way—"I see Rich has been busy doing some really original market analysis." This makes it difficult for your boss not to promote you if they want to win their peer group approval. If the other bosses think you are a good idea then your boss really has to go along with it.

Underpromise and Overdeliver

If you know you can do it by Wednesday always say Friday. If you know it will take your department a week, say two. If you know it will cost an extra two people to get the new machine installed and up and running, then say three.

This isn't dishonest, merely prudent. If it gets spotted that this is what you do, then openly and honestly admit it and say you always build in a contingency percentage into your calculations. They can't kill you for that.

That's the first part. Underpromise. And just because you have said Friday or two weeks or whatever doesn't mean you can coast and use up that allowance. Oh, no. What you have to do is make sure you deliver early, on budget, and better than promised. And that's the second part. Overdeliver. This means if you promised to have the report finished by Monday, first thing, it is finished but not only is it a report but it also contains the full implementation plans for the new premises. Or if you said you'd have the exhibition stand up and running by Sunday night with only two extra members of staff you have—and you've managed to get your major competitor to pull out of the show. Or if you said you'd have a rough proposal written for the new company brochure by the next meeting you not only have this but also a full color mock-up, the complete text written and proofread, all the photos taken and full printing costs and quotes for distribution. Obviously you've got to be careful that you don't overstep the mark and assume responsibilities you haven't been given, but I'm sure you get the idea.

Again it might be stating the obvious but don't be too blatant when you do this or your boss will get to expect it—it should be a pleasant surprise not a frequently used tactic.

It also helps sometimes to act dumb. You can pretend you don't really understand some new technique or software when in reality you know it back to front. Then when you suddenly do all the budgets on the spreadsheets that no one else could, you look good. If, in advance, you had said "Oh, yes, I know that, I worked with these spreadsheets at my last place," there is no surprise and you've given the game away—and your advantage.

When you underpromise and overdeliver you have to have a bottom line—in your case, as a Rules Player, it is simply that you will never deliver late or deliver short. That's it. If you have to sweat blood and work all night then so be it. You will deliver when you said you would—or earlier if you can—without exception. It is better to negotiate a longer delivery time in the first place than to have to let someone down. A lot of people are so keen to be liked, or approved of, or praised that they will agree to the first delivery time offered to them—"Oh yes, I can do that," and then they fail. They look like pushovers in the first place and incompetent in the end.

Know Something Others Don't

I once worked with a guy called Steve who knew as much French, probably, as the rest of us, but who saw it as an opportunity to have something no one else did. He went to evening classes, went on holiday to France every year, listened to French records, and read French novels. Within a very short time he was fluent, very good. He had also, accurately, predicted that we were going into Europe and his knowledge of French became a very valuable asset indeed. Knowing something that other people don't know gives you an edge—and it's that edge that you're looking for. Steve did it with language—using it to carve out a niche—but you can do it with skills, talents, expertise, aptitude, or flair.

First you have to look at your talents—and this is part of *Rule 37: Know Your Strengths and Weaknesses*—and decide where specialist knowledge could be useful. Perhaps you're a wizard with computers or other technology. Maybe you are very creative and could usefully know a lot that others don't. I had a friend who knew the print business inside and out, when printing work was needed it was always to her that the bosses went. This gave her, her edge.

How about finance? Could you interpret the business pages for others? Or how about being the one who really understands the budget? Or futures? Or software installation? Or contracts? Or staff issues? Or union laws? Or health and safety? Or foreign customs and business practices? Or currency conversions? Or body language? Or team building? Or chairing meetings really well? Or. Or. Or. Come on, you have to do some of this as well. I'm not going to give you all my best ideas.

Whatever it is you decide upon make sure it is:

- Relevant
- Topical
- Interesting.

That way others will come to you when they have need of your services. If you know something they don't you become a consultant rather than a mere employee. Obviously, if it is something your boss needs that's all the better.

I worked with one guy who had made it his business to know the local nightlife better than the rest of us—restaurants, nightclubs, theaters, that sort of thing. It seemed a bit irrelevant at first, but when we started talking to a lot of clients from out of town who needed to stay over, he certainly made his mark. Guess who was called in to show them around in the evenings and thus was part of the wining-and-dining circuit? Yep. And, of course, once in with the bosses at that level, it wasn't long before he too was one of them.

Be 100 Percent Committed

Being a Rules Player means you are going to have to work a whole lot harder than any of your colleagues. They can coast, you can't. They can afford to lighten up and put their feet up, you can't. To get on and up you have to be 100 per cent committed. You can't afford to lose sight of your long-term goal for a second. For you there is no time off, no downtime, no lounging around time, no slip ups, no mistakes, no accidental deviations from the script.

You have to become like a master criminal—they lead incredibly law-abiding lives because they can't risk breaking a tiny law in case it draws attention to themselves and the really big crimes get revealed—and watch what you say and what you do.

If any of this seems too much then bow out now. I only want committed Rules Players on this team. You are going to have to sign an oath in blood if you want to make this grade. You are going to have to be vigilant, dedicated, watchful, keen, ready, prepared, cautious, alert, and on the ball. Tall order.

Is it worth it? You bet. In the land of the blind, you will be the only one with both eyes open and seeing. You will be powerful—and most importantly you will be having fun. There is no greater buzz than seeing the games that are going on around you and being completely uninvolved, utterly objective, and supremely detached.

You will find that you won't have to do very much once you start observing. You will be able to give people a tiny nudge to get them to change direction rather than a huge big shove. Your dealings become incredibly delicate and gentle.

But you really do have to be 100 percent committed. If you try this stuff without such dedication you will go off half-cocked and run the risk of looking foolish instead of cool and in control. But the beauty of total commitment is that you no longer have any decisions to make. You know exactly your path and in any situation you only have to ask "Does this further my Rule playing or not?"—and then the decision is made for you. Easy.

> ## "YOU ARE GOING TO HAVE TO BE VIGILANT, DEDICATED, WATCHFUL, KEEN, READY, PREPARED, CAUTIOUS, ALERT, AND ON THE BALL."

Enjoy What You Are Doing

If you're not enjoying yourself, what are you doing? If there is no entertainment value in your work then there really is no point in doing it—you can probably get enough somewhere else to survive. I think there are an awful lot of people out there who really do enjoy working but are frightened to say so in case they get accused of being workaholics or sad or something.

There is no shame in saying you enjoy your work. There seems to be some kudos in being miserable at work, in moaning about your situation. There is a sort of office pecking order where people try to outdo each other in moaning about how much they hate their work.

Not for you there's not. The Rules Player enjoys work and makes sure people know that. Once you acknowledge that work is fun—and for you it is even more fun than for anyone else—you will find your step lightens, your stress levels decrease, and your whole demeanor lightens. By admitting work is fun you are trading in a secret bit of knowledge that only really successful people usually have. Work is fun—engrave it on your heart.

> ## "THERE IS NO SHAME IN SAYING YOU ENJOY YOUR WORK."

Having a good time at work and realizing work is good isn't the same thing. Work being good means you take pride in what you do, enjoy the challenge, look forward to each day with optimism and enthusiasm. Having a good time at work means not achieving much, talking a lot, making fun of colleagues, and drinking champagne all afternoon. There is a difference I'm sure you will agree. Having a good time at work is a temporary thing. It lasts while the fun lasts but quickly flags once the excitement, the elation has worn off.

Work being good means enjoying the negotiating, the hiring and firing, the day-to-day challenges, the stresses and disappointments, the uncertain future, the testing of one's mettle, the new learning curves. A surprising number of people die within a year of retirement—this suggests that it's more important to our existence than we think.

If you ain't enjoying all this and appreciating that it is enjoyable then you are doomed to be one of the moaners, one of life's victims.

RULE 9

Develop the Right Attitude

At work a lot of people have a sort of "us and them" attitude. They like to side with the "workers" and moan about the "management." You, on the other hand, will develop the right attitude and not become one of the "us" mentality. No matter what your position now, you are the next head of department, an embryonic chairman of the board, a budding managing director. You have to start to look at both sides of a situation and identify the position of "them." You may not voice this and may even, in public, appear to side with your fellow workers and colleagues. But deep down, in your heart, you understand and side with "them." Never forget that. Your colleagues may moan about management policy, but you will analyze it and try to see it from their point of view. To fit in and blend you may be tempted to adopt the camouflage of a moaning worker—not a wise move. Nod in agreement but don't moan yourself.

The right attitude is twofold:

- First you side with management and see policy decision from their point of view.
- Second you devote your attention to becoming a total and committed Rules Player—you look out for Number One (that's you).

The right attitude means giving it your best shot, not just today but every day. Not just when it's easy but when it's really hard as well.

The right attitude means going that extra mile, giving it that extra effort even when you're tired and angry and ready to quit. Others can quit, you can't, you're a Rules Player.

The right attitude is head up, never moaning, always positive and upbeat, constantly looking for the advantage and the edge.

The right attitude is developing standards—and sticking to them. Being sure of your bottom line and knowing when to make a stand. The right attitude is being aware that you have enormous power and that you will exercise that power with kindness, restraint, humanity and consideration. You won't put anyone down or be ruthless or manipulative. Yes, you may take advantage of others' sleepiness or apathy or wrong attitude—that's their problem. But you will take the moral high ground and be blameless. The right attitude is being good but quick, kind but observant, considerate but successful.

Never Let Anyone Know How Hard You Work

Look at someone like Richard Branson. He is always seen as playing, flying balloons, living on a converted barge, flying to the United States. You never see him sitting at a desk, answering phones, doing paperwork. But at some time during his working day that is exactly what he must do. We just don't get to see it. Thus we think of him as the business playboy, the happy-go-lucky entrepreneur, the devilish entertainer. It's a neat image and one that he seems very happy to go along with—and why not?

This is the sort of image the intrepid Rules Player wants to cultivate—suave, easy, relaxed, languid, in control, and very chilled. You never run, never panic, never even seem to hurry. Yes, you may stay up until the early hours of every morning but you will never admit this. Yes, you may work through your vacation, weekends and days off, but you will never let on, never moan about how hard you work or the hours you put in. To the outside observer you are coasting, taking it easy, taking it all in your stride.

Obviously to be able to do this you have to be very good at your job. If you ain't, then you're going to fail big time trying this rule out for size. So, what do you do if you aren't very good at your job? Burn that midnight oil again getting good. Learn, study, gain experience and knowledge, read, ask questions until you do know that job inside and out. Do this first and then you can swan about looking cool and very relaxed.

There are a few rules within this rule:

- Never ask for an extension of a deadline.
- Never ask for help: never admit that you are out of your depth—you can ask for guidance, advice, information, an opinion, but never help.
- Never moan or complain about how much work you have to do.
- Learn to be assertive so you don't get overloaded—this is not about letting others know how hard you do work, but you don't have to overdo it and overwork.
- Never be seen breaking into a sweat.
- Always look for ways to ease your workload—unnoticed of course—and ways to speed things up.

KNOW THAT YOU'RE BEING JUDGED AT ALL TIMES

Everything about us speaks volumes to others. The way we dress, the car we drive, where we go on vacation, how we talk and walk, what we eat at lunchtime—everything about us is subject to the judgment of others.

Part 2 is making sure that the judgment is positive and enhances your career. If you've never thought about it before, this rule will help you recognize the signals you give off and how to improve them so others take notice. You can't stop people making judgments—but you can change those judgments and consciously affect them. This rule is about being stylish, confident, smart, well groomed and very smooth.

RULE 11

Dress Well

Dress well means exactly that—dress well. There is simply no excuse for dressing badly, dressing down, dressing dumb, dressing cheaply, or dressing carelessly.

I'm afraid that this rule is very important and must be strictly adhered to. There are no days off, no excuses, no letters from your mother letting you off. Dressing well is the most noticeable thing about you. If you relax your guard for a moment it will be remembered. On the other hand, it might be a lot less work never to embark on this one and remain unpromoted, unsuccessful, unpowerful because once you start you can't let up for a second.

So what do we mean by well? Simply that, well. For a man it might mean a suit, collar and tie and polished leather shoes. For a woman it could mean an elegant two-piece business suit, smart hosiery, sensible shoes. On the other hand, you may need to tone this down, if your company dress code is permanently casual, *see Rule 53* but the cheaply and badly rules still apply.

If you are in any doubt here is a simple checklist of don'ts:

- No tennis shoes
- No blue jeans
- No Hawaiian, or any other fancy style or type, shirts

- No Velcro, no manufactured (what used to be known as "man-made") fabrics such as nylon etc., no "state-of-the-art" articles, no modern fashions, no extremes, no statements of artistic licence

I used to watch a young man come to work. He was efficient, experienced, clever, a good communicator, reliable, trustworthy and honest, diligent and presentable—but he wasn't getting promoted. Why not? Because he was ignoring Rule 11. Oh yes, he dressed well enough at work. It was his arrival that was wrong. He rode a motorcycle. Nothing wrong with that. It saved him money and made sure he didn't get stuck in traffic jams—highly commendable. But it was holding him back. As he walked through the office each morning he clutched his motorcycle helmet and wore an all-in-one bright orange motorcycle suit. Again highly commendable. It made sure he could be seen even on foggy mornings and was hard wearing and protective in the event of an accidental spill. But it also drew attention to him as a "youth." Middle managers don't ride motorcycles. Senior executives have long since given up the Harley lust. So this young man wasn't going to get promoted while he "looked" like a biker, in any shape or form. Once I got him to take the orange suit off before he came into the office and leave the helmet in reception, he was away and his rise up the ladder was meteoric. He didn't have to give up the motorcycle, just stop advertising the fact he was still young enough to ride one.

RULE 12

Cultivate a Smile

Remember the poem? If you can keep your head etc.—well, how do you let them know you are keeping your head? Easy, smile. Smile no matter what. Smile when you greet your colleagues in the morning. Smile when you shake hands. Smile when it's getting tough. Smile when it's hell. Smile no matter what.

And what sort of smile? Friendly, genuine—make sure it extends to your eyes—sincere, frank, honest, open, happy. And the easiest way to make your smile all these things is to believe them all. This can't be an act or it'll be spotted immediately. It has to be genuine to appear genuine. You have to feel happy. You have to be enjoying this or your smile will look insincere and false. And if you're not enjoying this then stop pretending with a fake smile and get the hell out.

We'll assume your smile is real and that it comes from genuine happiness and friendliness. Now it is legit to improve on your smile, to rehearse it, to make it better. But it has to be there in the first place. We'll assume it is.

Look in the mirror and smile. Chances are it will look all wrong. Of course it will. You can only see yourself head on. And photos don't work either, they're in 2D and there is a lot missing when you look at them. You need to see your smile from all angles, in 3D, and there is only one way to see this and that is on film—video or whatever.

If you feel embarrassed getting a partner or friend to video you so you can improve your smile then you'll have to set it up yourself. Please don't make the mistake I once made. I was a finance manager and was asked to cover for one of our super-market managers for an afternoon. The store was empty and I spent a most enjoyable afternoon practicing my walk, my smile, my general appearance on the video surveillance system in the store. I would go back to the office and watch the results as I changed a slight part of whatever bit I was unhappy with. It was great fun. A few weeks later I was invited to watch a special show for all the staff. Yes, I had forgotten to erase the tape and the shop manager had found it and had been putting on shows for all the general staff. I was forced to sit through the whole thing while my laughing friends commented on it and pointed out where I was going wrong. Very horrible, but very funny.

So to improve your smile make sure you aren't doing a lopsided grin, that your teeth can be seen but not too much, that you look happy and honest. Keep practicing until you get it right.

No Limp Fish— Develop the Perfect Handshake

We shake hands often and usually quite unconsciously. How many times do you have to shake hands during a normal business week? And how much thought do you give to it? There are so many signals given during that brief handshake though, that you really ought to make it supremely confident, utterly secure, and convincingly reassuring. When someone shakes hands with you they should be left with the impression of strength, confidence, power, and of someone totally in control of themselves—that's you of course. If you are in any doubt about the "rightness" of your handshake get a friend to tell you.

How do you make it better? Make it firm. You can always use the other hand to reassuringly grip both your hand and that of your boss/colleague/client. But don't overdo it and leave them with crushed fingers.

You can always adapt your handshake to make it more individual, more memorable. My grandfather had a wonderful handshake, he just used his first two fingers (the fore and index) and his thumb and gripped very firmly. You felt as if you were shaking hands with royalty.

Handshakes are very formal, old-fashioned things. Forget about the high fives, the Masonic twitches or anything gangsta-style. Stick to the old-fashioned sort of shake and you will be remembered as someone confident and authoritative.

Good shakers are the ones who proffer their hand first as well as shaking well. They exude confidence by announcing their name and offering their hand at the same time thus showing keenness, friendliness, a relaxed and confident approach, and a general air of assertiveness. They also look you in the eyes and say your name back to you. We like hearing our own name and it's a memory enhancer.

When you do announce your name the word that goes first is "Hello." That's it. You might like to be modern and friendly and say "Hi"—that's up to you. But the good Rules Player says "Hello." And follows that with their name. And your name is also formal and old fashioned. It is *never* "Hi, I'm Dave, from Marketing." The effect is pleasant enough and certainly friendly, but you will have impressed no one, gained no benefit or advantage and brought yourself down to just about the level of the most junior person there. Much better to say "Hello, I'm David Simpson, Marketing Manager." This immediately separates you from the herd and makes you more senior to anyone else there. Follow this up with a firm, confident handshake and you will have them eating out of your hand.

Exude Confidence and Energy

I once had to give a talk to a large group of businesswomen about stress management. As I walked to the front to start my talk, I noticed that there was no lectern for notes (not that I had any anyway), nowhere to stand. There was a desk with a chair behind it. If I sat there I would have been lost to view to anyone who wasn't in the front row and it would have seemed very stilted and formal. I could have stood there with my arms behind my back looking like Prince Philip talking to the palace staff. I could have stood there with my hands by my side or clasped in front of my groin like an embarrassed schoolboy. But I was about to talk about stress—and its management. I needed to look relaxed, calm—as if I was practicing what I was preaching, walking my talk.

I solved it by sitting on the edge of the desk. I could swing my legs, lean back, lean forward, almost lie down if I wanted. I met someone several years later who had been there and she said that she couldn't remember a thing I'd said, but had been impressed by how relaxed I'd seemed—and how when I'd finished talking I sprang up and went off for photos with the

> ## "WHEN YOU WALK THROUGH THE OFFICE FIRST THING IN THE MORNING THERE SHOULD BE A SPRING TO YOUR STEP."

local journalist. I don't remember that bit but she said I seemed confident, relaxed but also energetic.

That's what we're aiming for. When you walk through the office first thing in the morning there should be a spring to your step. Let the others crawl in looking hung over or fresh out of bed or exhausted from long hours commuting. You will arrive fresh and energetic, ready for the day's work which shall be as a trifle to you to deal with, a mere nothing. Walk quicker rather than slower—quick means keen, means energy, means awake and lively and ready for the challenges the day will throw your way.

Not too quick mind or you'll seem to be in a rush. You need to be smoothly in control—not hurried, not sluggardly, not cowed or beaten. You need to be seen as bright and fresh and alive and enthusiastic.

Develop a Style That Gets You Noticed

The word is "style." That means tasteful, formal, civilized, sophisticated, elegant, cultured, refined, and discerning. You are going to develop a style that gets you noticed in all these things. Dyeing your hair red and only ever wearing clothes from Goodwill may indeed be a style and one that does get you noticed, but it's not for the Rules Player. Think Cary Grant rather than Boy George. Think Lauren Bacall rather than Madonna. All have style, all attracted attention. But trust me, Cary or Lauren is what you want. Classic, timeless, quality. You have various options if you want to adopt a style:

- Choose one thing and get known for it—always wear black, or double breasted, or Armani, or have a classy handbag/briefcase collection. Develop a trademark dress style—and stick to it.

- Only ever buy the very best you can afford.

- Never wear anything tight—loose clothes talk of quality and elegance, tight clothes of poverty and cheapness.

- Less is more—cut down on jewellery and buy/wear only the very best, the finest. If it's not expensive then don't wear it. You'll find that if you only limit yourself to very expensive items it helps you eliminate anything that might be considered dubious or of questionable taste—spending a lot makes you much more discriminating.

- If you wear makeup then stick to what suits you, what makes you look good. Don't change your makeup with the seasons or with what's in vogue—be known for your look, be instantly recognizable, be stylish.

- Always dress up rather than down—formal is best, informal is worst.

- Make sure all accessories follow the same rules as your dress sense—stylish, expensive, loose, recognizable, tasteful. There's not a lot of point in looking good and then dragging round a battered old briefcase that's seen better days—not unless, of course, that's your trademark in which case make sure the briefcase is very old and very battered and very expensive.

> ## "THINK CARY GRANT RATHER THAN BOY GEORGE. THINK LAUREN BACALL RATHER THAN MADONNA."

Pay Attention to Personal Grooming

Each and every morning you need to check that your personal grooming is in tip-top condition. Details really matter. You let one thing go and it will be noticed—and it could be the one thing that makes the vital difference between a promotion and a rejection. Make each day as conscientious as an interview day. Before you leave for work check:

- Shoes shined and in good repair.
- Clothes pressed, clean, new, in good condition—no buttons off, no rips, tears, or splits.
- You are freshly showered, deodorant in place.
- Hair clean every day—and well cut and styled on a regular and consistent basis.
- Men shaved—if you have to have facial hair check for straggly hairs, crumbs, insects, fluff.
- Women made up—this can be as simple as you want but it must be good, consistent and perfect.
- Teeth clean and in good repair, breath fresh, tongue clean (no yellow fur).
- Nails clean and freshly manicured.

> # "MAKE EACH DAY
> # AS CONSCIENTIOUS
> # AS AN
> # INTERVIEW DAY."

- Hands clean and no ingrained grime from working on old cars or DIY or gardening—wear thin surgical gloves for all those dirty jobs.

- If you smoke/drink a lot of coffee make sure your teeth aren't stained (or hands for smokers) and use mints/chewing gum to avoid dog breath.

- Nose (and ear) hair tidied up/removed.

- If you wear glasses make sure they suit you, are renewed on a yearly basis so that you can see, that they are a perfect fit and that they are in good condition—no cracked lenses or taped repairs.

You don't have to become vain or to keep checking yourself in the mirror. Once you have got it right, relax and enjoy it. I worked with a woman who would go and clean her teeth after every coffee or donut. Nothing wrong with that except it drew attention to herself and her colleagues thought her strange and obsessive. Her fault was not in cleaning her teeth so often but in making such a song and dance out of it. A little discretion would have been much better.

RULE 17

Be Attractive

There is no doubt about it, and statistics back it up, handsome people get on better than those less fortunate. Handsome people have to work less hard to get on. But what makes someone attractive, handsome? If you look at someone you consider attractive, you will be hard pressed to see what it is that they've got that makes them so good looking. Attractiveness, if we ignore the obvious physical impairments such as buck teeth or a warty nose—all of which can be corrected—is very hard to define. Take any Hollywood star, such as Liza Minelli, Woody Allen, Julie Roberts, Sean Penn, who aren't classically good looking and we can see that they have charisma, charm, magnetism, a larger-than-life attitude. They come right out at you. They have life, presence, drama, power, and personality.

You too must have these things. They are easier to acquire than looks anyway. Being attractive is all part of the rules in Part 2. If you dress well, pay attention to your grooming, cultivate that smile, look good and cool at all times and come across as friendly, warm, articulate and caring you will also come across as attractive and good looking. Looks are all in the smile and the eyes. Smiles that light up a room are magnetic and powerful. Eyes that twinkle and are full of life are enough to make us think the whole face is good looking.

Attractiveness is also about posture and position. If you slump you give off an aura of gloom and depression. This is unattractive and not good looking.

Your walk should be erect, proud, assured. So should your handshake. Everything about you should be up and open, happy and confident. This is attractive. Your grooming should be faultless, your dress sense superb, your style quirky but suave, your whole demeanor splendid and outstanding. This is attractive.

You do not:

- Slouch
- Slump
- Be scruffy

You do:

- Get anything fixed that can be fixed that would be considered unattractive—warts, bad breath, bad teeth, poor eyesight (Stop squinting for God's sake and get some proper glasses!)

RULE 18

Be Cool

You don't necessarily wear green on St. Patrick's Day. You don't dress up in costume no matter what. You don't alter your impeccable style for anything or anyone. You remain aloof from all that office nonsense. Will this get you a reputation as standoffish? Arrogant? Self-important? Who cares? It will make you cool and that is all that is important. Save the theatrics for the weekends when it doesn't matter who sees you. Remain civilized and sophisticated at all times.

Let's face it—you are there to do a job. That's what they pay you for. You ain't there to make a fool of yourself. Just so long as you do that job—and do it well—the way you do it is up to you. You can choose to get involved in all the social side of the office or you can remain one step removed. This makes you one step away from your colleagues and thus one step nearer to being their manager.

None of this means you can't have a laugh and joke with your work mates, just don't get so friendly or personal that it would become impossible to promote you above them. If you are going to be their boss soon then it pays to keep a little bit of distance. And you do this by being cool.

If you don't know what cool is try typing in cool into your word processor and then using the Thesaurus option look for antonyms. You get: warm, excited, unfashionable. For warm think sweaty hands—uncool. For excited think small boy on

> # "REMAIN CIVILIZED
> # AND
> # SOPHISTICATED
> # AT ALL TIMES."

Christmas Day—cute but uncool. For unfashionable think chunky cardigans—warm and uncool.

So we want to be:

- Not warm—think not sweaty.
- Not excited—think not panicked.
- Not unfashionable—this isn't the same as fashionable but rather a timeless stylishness, which is, of course, completely different.

The cool operator is relaxed and in control. In a crisis they don't rush about screaming, but rather implement safety procedures and calmly and smoothly handle the situation. They are cool. They keep their heads and their composure. And invariably these are the people who others will turn to in a difficult situation. You don't want someone who panics, you want someone cool, calm, and collected.

RULE 19

Speak Well

So what does speaking well mean? Am I suggesting you walk around with a Boston Brahmin voice and say "rother" instead of "rather?" Of course not. You can keep your regional accent; that's not the problem. Look at *why* we speak—it is to communicate, to convey information—rather than *how* we speak. Speaking well means getting information over clearly and effectively. It doesn't matter *how* you speak, but it does matter that you speak clearly. And speaking clearly means just that—clearly. The things you must avoid are:

- Mumbling—For obvious reasons, they can't hear or understand you.
- Speaking too softly or quietly—Again they can't hear you.
- Using jargon—It's unintelligible to others outside of your department or field of expertise.
- Any sort of speaking that identifies you with a particular group or social class—i.e. youth (trying to use the latest trendy slang or catchphrase), or politically extreme (radical anything, politically correct gone mad, ecologist, vegetarian or environmentally obsessive), or too obviously belonging to any class system (too aristocratic, too low class, too regional).

Speaking badly—using "less" when you really mean "fewer"—that sort of thing. If you don't know the difference get an

English grammar book and learn it by heart. Don't use verbal mannerisms such as "you know" or "like." Always finish your sentences.

There are four key words to remember to get you speaking well:

- Bright
- Clear
- Pleasant
- Simple

That's all you need to know. If you use these four, you won't go wrong and people will remember what you say and be impressed by your clear, bright speaking voice. Speaking well makes an impact. If you slouch in and mumble your name people will assume you are under-confident, ill at ease, and barely human—and thus quickly forget you. If you walk in confidently, say your name clearly and with confidence people will assume you know where you are going, who you are and what you want—and thus remember you. Speak simply—say directly what it is you want to say, and nothing more.

Write Well

We write for two purposes. We write for others to read and we write for ourselves to read. How you write for yourself is immaterial. You can scribble illegible shorthand or write like a five-year-old. It doesn't matter, just so long as no one else sees it. But how you write for others to read is of utmost and crucial importance. You will be judged on:

- What you write
- How your writing looks

Ah, but you say you don't write anything, you type everything. Fine. So what type face do you choose, and why? What point size, and why? And you must have to sign documents—that's writing. Your signature is as open to judgment as anything else. I was once told that my signature was that of a very wealthy person. Good, although completely wrong, but it did indicate that I was getting close to the image I wanted to portray. A final point on this: always make your signature big—big signature, big person.

If you use handwriting a lot then it needs to be:

- Legible—It must be able to be read by everyone—or there simply is no point doing it and it is discourteous not to make the effort.
- Neat—No crossings out, all lines equal, that sort of thing.
- Stylish—A bit of a flourish here and there.

- Mature—Cursive, with nice rounded letters.

- Consistent—The writing at the bottom of the page should look like the writing at the top of the page.

Watch your margins and slope of your writing. You may not know it but margins—or signatures or any form of writing—that slopes down toward the right of the page indicate a depressed person. Optimists slant upward.

Make sure your spelling is correct and your grammar adequate—if not make it so.

If you type a lot, use Times New Roman or Arial, 12 point and only use *italics* or **bold** or <u>underlining</u> sparingly. Never mix **type faces** – it betrays you as an unstable, immature personality, apparently—or point size. And you just thought it looked fun.

> ## "HOW YOU WRITE FOR OTHERS TO READ IS OF UTMOST AND CRUCIAL IMPORTANCE."

PART 3

HAVE A PLAN

Do you know where you're going? If you don't, then the probability is that you'll end up going nowhere. The smart follower of *The Rules* knows exactly where they're going. They have a plan. They have plotted the path to where they want to be—in six months, in a year, in five years. They've planned their game and know how to play. And so will you. Rules Players remain flexible and convert their plan according to circumstances—they're not rigid thinkers but smart and very fluid.

RULE 21

Know What You Want Long Term

So what's your game plan for your life? Don't know? Haven't ever thought about it? Most people don't. And that's why they fail. If you don't have a plan it is terribly easy not to stick to it and end up where the current takes you—a bit of flotsam adrift on the eddies of life, very sad. The Rules Player has a plan—long term and short term.

Long-term plans can be very simple—qualify, move up, reach the top, retire, die. Or they can be sensible and useful. If you intend to have a career it makes sense to study the game plan of your chosen industry. Obviously you will have to build in a certain contingency for the unexpected and the "out-of-your-control," but the shrewd Rules Player will have already amended their long-term game plan well in advance having seen the indicators and read the signs. I spoke to someone recently who said, "Who would have predicted downsizing then?" The answer is anyone with the brains to have seen which way their business sector was going.

So study your chosen industry and see the progression steps needed to make it to the position you want to occupy. Work out what you need to make those steps. Work out how many steps it takes—usually no more than about four—junior, middle, senior, executive. (If you think otherwise don't write in.)

Work out what you want from each step—gaining experience, handling responsibility, learning new skills, acquiring people-management understanding, that sort of thing. You will notice that "increasing my earnings" just isn't an option here—that is a foregone conclusion if you are a Rules Player anyway.

Work out how each step is made. This might be a transfer to another department, relocation to another branch, being offered a partnership, being invited to join the board, moving to another company, that sort of thing. Once you know *how* each step is made, it doesn't take much to work out what you need to acquire that *how*.

You have to have an end game—the final goal. This can be as high or as extreme as you like—emperor of the world, president, CEO, wealthiest person in the world, whatever. It is a dream and thus has no limits. If you set limits on your imagination, then you will have to settle for less than the best, less than perfect, less than you deserve. Ah, but you say we have to be realistic. Fine, do that, be realistic. But a Rules Player heads for the very utmost of their dreams and nothing less than the top is good enough.

Know What You Want Short Term

How short is short term? That's entirely up to you. I have three short-term plans on the go—this month, this year, five years. This seems to provide me with sufficient information to plan my workload. It also allows me to work in, in the short term, plans that affect my family. I can allow for vacations, changes of school, garden/house projects, and birthdays, Christmas, that sort of thing.

- Your one-month short-term plan should obviously list current work projects—deadlines, prioritized tasks, basic routines. This is for work actually being carried out.

- Your one-year plan should have projects which are being formulated, planned, presented, whatever. This is for work being planned rather than executed.

- Your five-year plan should be for ideas, dreams, goals, wishes, wants, it is for work you intend executing one day.

Your long-term plan will have a career path built in to it. Your five-year plan will take into it any steps you need to carry out that long-term plan.

I tend to keep three separate records for these three short-term plans. My one-month plan is kept on a clipboard on the desk. It contains a single sheet which lists boxes for deadlines, return phone calls, things to do. I suppose it's a bit like a calendar but without daily entries.

My one-year plan lives on the wall. It isn't a wall chart or year planner but again a single sheet with twelve boxes. In each box is a month with the relevant info of what I want to do during that time. It is what I *want* to do rather than what I *have* to do. It is a short-term plan not a to-do list or a calendar or a work schedule. As I am a freelancer I have to generate work. This work—being done during my one-month plan or being generated during my one-year plan—is my bread and butter. It is made up of projects I want to do and projects I have to do. The ones I *have* to do are the bread and the ones I *want* to do are the butter—such as this book which has been a delight to plan and write. My five-year plan is for my general direction— what sort of work do I want to be doing over the next five years? Your short-term plan will include work you have to do, but it will be mainly for work you want to do. The shorter the term, the more likely it is to read like your work schedule and less like a wish list.

All plans should include practical steps to put into action and make them happen. Otherwise they aren't "plans" but vague ideas.

Within any of these plans you have to build a contingency. Someone phones you up with a project, you can't turn it down on the basis that it isn't in your plan. You have to be flexible.

Study the Promotion System

When you start your career, it is at the lowest level and you gaze upward at the boss, the manager, the managing director, with reverence and awe. One day, inevitably, you will age, gain experience, and ascend to greater heights yourself. Either that or maybe start up on your own. And for most people that's about it. Career-wise they meander vaguely upward, often getting sidetracked and stopping at a level where they seem comfortable, coasting, happy. And that's it. Career over. Game over. Very sad. Unless that's really what you want. And if you're a committed Rules Player, I doubt it.

The Rules Player never meanders or arrives anywhere vaguely. You plan. You know the system and use it. You understand the steps to be taken to get you from A to B and onward and upward all the way to Z.

You have to study the promotion system if you are to enter it and profit from it. It is simply no use waiting for something to turn up, or for fate to take a hand and propel you upward by luck or chance. You have to seize the day and make your own luck. You have to know exactly how to avoid all clichés and elevate yourself within the system.

So, what is the promotion system within your industry? Do you know it? Have you studied it? Study the background of others who have been there before you. If not chances are you are relying on luck to get you somewhere. This may be fine and it may get you where you want to be but it is unreliable—bit like playing the lottery in the hope it'll make you rich and you can retire. It might happen but it's not likely.

Making a promotion chart:

- Within your industry look upward to the most senior position that can be held (or the highest you could possibly expect yourself to aim for, they should really be the same thing—mark this).
- Now look at the lowest—mark this.
- Now plot all the steps in-between.
- Now mark your own place.
- Now list the steps needed to get there.

You now have your own promotion chart and can cross off each step as you make it.

(The same principle of steps also works if you decide that rather than ascend where you are, you'd like to set up on your own and be entrepreneurial rather than corporate.)

While you are doing this, you can also list all the skills/ experience etc. that you would need for each step to be made successfully. Next to this, you can add what you have to do to acquire these—where you must go, what you have to learn, what you need to study. You can add these back into your long-term plan and your five-year plan.

Develop a Game Plan

Developing a game plan is a bit like an actor choosing a part and learning their script. Your game plan has to be who you are going to be. Not many people choose consciously to be a loser but that's where they end up. Don't let it happen to you. And it doesn't happen, once you seize the initiative and develop a game plan.

Your game plan is a sort of personal mission statement. It is different from setting objectives which is how to be the person your game plan decides you are.

So who are you going to be? Successful? A failure? Someone who gives up? Someone who picks themselves up, dusts themselves off, and starts all over again? A brilliant career strategist? A loser? None of these?

Obviously you could decide to be ruthless, unpleasant, cruel, vindictive, but we assume you won't—a Rules Player is never any of these. Your game plan should include your qualities as well as what sort of game you want to plan—"I will be successful and still be a thoroughly nice person."

Not many people sit down and consciously carry out this exercise. It may seem simple but it is an essential tool to get you to where you want to be. If more people did this they wouldn't end up as idiots, or the office bore, or a gossip, or frighteningly callous in their dealings with their colleagues. If we all had to sit down and write our game plan—and then live by it—we might all end up as nicer people. There is no bad karma in trying your hardest to be pleasant, cooperative, helpful, friendly, kind, and honest in your dealings with others around you. Who would sit down and write, "I am going to be a complete and utter bastard and aggravate as many people as I can, be disliked by everyone and generally make myself as unpopular as possible?" Yes, no one would write it, but I've worked with quite a few who live by it as a game plan. Yes, they may be successful but how do they sleep at night? How do they live with themselves?

I once worked with a fairly senior manager whose technique was to arrive, walk through the department, bawl out as many people as he could, go to his office, put his feet up with a coffee for half an hour, and then walk back again being as nice as pie to everyone. When I questioned him about this, he said, "It keeps them on their toes. They never know where they are with me." He was genuinely disliked by everyone, feared by most and commanded zero respect from his peers. Good game plan. Not.

RULE 25

Set Objectives

An objective is a simple one-sentence mission statement that you can use to get you through your day. It is almost impossible to be successful or to get promoted if you don't set objectives.

An objective outlines the key, important, ingredients in your work recipe. Suppose you have a meeting to go to. Now we all hate meetings, they are interminable, boring, unproductive, counterproductive—and an endless source of irritation and argument. You know that Stephen from accounts is going to be there and will endeavor—usually successfully—to get on your nerves. You know you'll get side-tracked and end up discussing the relocation to Cleveland when it doesn't even affect your department. You know you'll end up discussing budgets for the exhibition stand when that's six months away and it hasn't even been decided that you're going to take a stand at the tradeshow this year. So, set an objective:

"I will only speak on matters I know about and understand and are relevant to me at this meeting and no matter what Stephen does I shall not rise to the bait."

Good. Now stick to it.

Suppose you have to present a report to the Finance Committee about the new costings of the wildflower meadow to go in front of head office's new buildings. You know the Finance Committee can waffle on for hours about irrelevant topics such as whether it is better to have oxeye daises or

> ## "IT IS ALMOST IMPOSSIBLE TO BE SUCCESSFUL OR TO GET PROMOTED IF YOU DON'T SET OBJECTIVES."

marsh buttercups and all you need to do is present them with the cost of seeds, mowing equipment and haymaking provisions without getting caught up in the minutiae of which flower is most attractive in spring. So, set an objective:

"I will present my report and, once comments have been made, will make my excuses and leave. If the committee insist on discussing matters that are irrelevant to my being there I shall assertively point this out and leave."

Good, now stick to it.

Use an objective for every area of your working life. They take but seconds but they do help highlight:

- What is wrong
- Solutions to what is wrong
- Action to be taken to correct what is wrong
- Ways to prevent the problem recurring

Know Your Role

What is your role? I know you are there to do a job, carry out a function, perform certain tasks, follow set procedures, and all that. But what is your role? This is a bit like setting a game plan. A game plan outlines what sort of working person you are going to be. A role is what sort of facilitator you will be. Will you be an ideas person? A moderator? A communicator? A diplomat? A task master? A motivator? Basically your role is how you fit into the team—and yes, we are all team players, we have to be in this day and age.

Dr Meredith Belbin has spent over 20 years researching the nature of team work in order to improve people's strengths. He has identified nine distinct team roles:

- The Plant—Original thinkers; they generate new ideas; they offer solutions to problems; they think in radically different ways, laterally, imaginatively.

- The Resource Investigator—Creative; they like to take ideas and run with them; they are extrovert and popular.

- The Coordinator—Highly disciplined and controlled; they can focus on objectives; they unify a team.

- The Shaper—They are very achievement orientated; they like to be challenged and to get results.

- The Monitor Evaluator—They analyze and balance and weigh; they are calm and detached; they are objective thinkers.

- The Team Worker—They are supportive and cooperative; they make good diplomats as they only want what is best for the team.

- The Implementer—They have good organizational skills; they display common sense; they like to get the job done.

- The Completer—They check details; they tidy up after them; they are painstakingly conscientious.

- The Specialist—They are dedicated to acquiring a specialized skill; they are extremely professional; they have drive and dedication.

So which are you? What role do you play in the team? Are you happy with your role? Can you change it?

"BASICALLY YOUR ROLE IS HOW YOU FIT INTO THE TEAM—AND YES, WE ARE ALL TEAM PLAYERS, WE HAVE TO BE IN THIS DAY AND AGE."

RULE 27

Know Yourself— Strengths and Weaknesses

If you are going to be a Rules Player you have to be incredibly objective about yourself. A lot of people can't do this, they can't turn the spotlight on themselves objectively enough or brightly enough to see themselves as others see them. And it's not just how others see us, it's also how we see ourselves. We all carry a mental image of ourselves—what we look like and sound like, what makes us tick; how we work—but how realistic is this image? I think I work creatively and eccentrically, others think I am messy and unorganized. Which is true? Which is the reality?

To know your strengths and weaknesses you first have to understand your role—the way you work. I might see being creative as a strength—lots of lovely ideas, no attention to detail, generating new projects rather than seeing them through or actually working on them—surely all these are strengths? Not if I am a Completer or Implementer they're not, then they are weaknesses. Instead my strengths would be perseverance, diligence, stickability, predictability, conformity, steadfastness, orderliness—yuk, surely these are weaknesses? You have to know your role first before you can make subjective judgments about strengths and weaknesses.

If in doubt make lists, that's what I always say. Write down what you think are your strengths and weaknesses. Show this list to a close friend who you do not work with. Ask for their objective evaluation. Now show it to someone you can trust who you do work with. Is there a difference in their evaluation of how close to the truth you are? Bet there is quite a difference. This is because the special skills you bring to friendships are quite different from the ones you bring to a work relationship.

This rule is about knowing your strengths and weaknesses, it isn't necessarily about improving them, eliminating them, working on them, changing them in any way. What we are is what we are and it is what we have to work with. You may well be disorganized, erratic, unpredictable—is this good or bad? It all depends on your role. You may need to change your role to suit your strengths and weaknesses better.

A lot of people think that identifying their strengths and weaknesses means they get to lose the bad stuff and only work with the good stuff. Not true. This isn't therapy. This is the real world. We all have weaknesses. The secret trick is learning to work with them rather than trying to be perfect, which is unrealistic and unproductive.

You might be able to find better uses for your weaknesses— but then they would become strengths, wouldn't they? Think about it.

Identify Key Times and Events

A cobra has a lot of power, a lot of venom, a lot of energy. But how often do you see one strike? Rarely. They only use all that power and energy when it is:

- Appropriate
- Meaningful
- Advantageous
- Beneficial
- Necessary
- Important

They strike when in danger or when they need to feed. The rest of the time you wouldn't know they were there. The rest of the time they don't even look like cobras. They don't display their hood except when they have to. You will become a cobra. There is no point using all your energy and power when it ain't necessary. What you have to do is identify the key times and events—then you strike.

A cobra's key times and events are fairly simple to identify—threat and hunger. But what are yours? Much more difficult.

> "THERE IS NO
> POINT USING
> ALL YOUR
> ENERGY AND
> POWER WHEN
> IT AIN'T
> NECESSARY."

There's not a lot of point burning all that midnight oil to produce a report that only a couple of your colleagues get to see and is then forgotten. Wait until it's the big report that's going straight to the desk of the Managing Director, that's the one that needs the cobra's striking force.

Of course a lot of people wait for the key time—the office party, the exhibition at a national tradeshow, the CEO's visit—and then they completely and utterly mess it up. They get drunk or flub their lines, they are late or sick, or appear with their flies undone or their dress tucked into the back of their underwear.

And key events? The presentation is a good one. Get it right and it's remembered. Get it wrong and it's you that is forgotten.

You don't get it wrong. Identify these times and events and shine at them. Be a cobra and strike when it is appropriate.

Anticipate Threats

Threats come at us from every quarter, every day—layoffs, downsizing, takeovers, vindictive colleagues, irascible bosses, new technology, new systems, new procedures. In fact entire books are devoted to threats—mostly from change—such as *Who Moved My Cheese* and *How To Handle Tough Situations At Work*. If we can think on our feet, stay out of ruts, be flexible and move fast, roll with the punches and go the distance, we will not only survive change but we shall also be contortionists and athletes of the highest order. Of course, we can't do all that. There will be times when the threat will overtake us and we get squashed. It happens to us all. There is no getting away from the fact that life gets fired at us at point-blank range and we rarely if ever get time to duck.

But a threat is always that. Once it becomes a reality we can deal with it. While it is still a threat it induces fear but can do no harm. Spotting which threat will turn into a reality is the skill. The talent. There are many threats and we can't react to all of them. There are fewer realities and we have to react to them.

It helps if we don't see threats as threats, but instead as opportunities. Each threat that becomes a reality is an opportunity to grow and change, adapt and rework our methods and style of management. If our attitude is positive we tend to see threats less as a negative thing and more as a positive thing—they bring us the chance to prove ourselves. If we never get challenged we will never improve.

I was once employed as a manager by a company which was taken over. The new bosses brought in their own managers and three of us were "downgraded"—demoted in other words. We had no choice—apart from walking out of course. I was, by this time, a committed Rules Player so I saw it as an opportunity to prove to the new bosses that I was good enough to be one of their managers and, three months later, I was back up there.

Of the other two, one eventually walked and one stayed "downgraded." They both bitched and moaned and felt the move was derogatory and demeaning and an insult. It probably was, but I didn't need to feel depressed about it. I needed to get back up there—upward and onward.

> ## "EACH THREAT THAT BECOMES A REALITY IS AN OPPORTUNITY TO GROW AND CHANGE."

RULE 30

Look for Opportunities

I know I've said have a plan—both long term and short term—but there do come times when plans have to be thrown out of the window. These are the opportunities. I had a friend who wasn't getting on particularly fast in his promotion plan. One day he found himself sharing a compartment on the train with his Chairman. This was his opportunity. He could have flubbed his lines, made a jackass of himself, or been too embarrassed or nervous to take the advantage. But he didn't do any of these things. He made his pitch perfectly. All he did was to chat informally but with the respect his Chairman warranted; show a keen grasp of the company's history, mission statement, and general aims; be presentable, smart and well spoken; express himself clearly and articulately; and, most importantly, didn't noticeably press his advantage—he knew when to shut up and back off. It certainly worked. His department head was told by the Chairman that she had a "Smart young man there, bring him on a bit, will you?" What choice did she have but to promote him?

That's seizing an opportunity. You can't write that into your plan and these moments will come along. When they do you must:

* Recognize them
* Play them well
* Be cool and suave

> "LEARN TO SEE OPPORTUNITIES AS BALLS—IF THEY GET THROWN YOUR WAY YOU HAVE BUT A SPLIT SECOND TO CATCH THEM."

What you mustn't do is:

- Fail to recognize the moment for what it is—a fleeting opportunity
- Panic
- Overplay your hand
- Get so excited you make an idiot of yourself

Learn to see opportunities as balls—if they get thrown your way you have but a split second to catch them. There is no time for asking questions, looking over your shoulder, weighing the pros and cons or dancing the foxtrot. You either catch the ball or you don't.

Spend a little time looking back at what opportunities you have missed—and what you would do if you had the same chance a second time. Would you react differently now? What did you do wrong?

PART 4

IF YOU CAN'T SAY ANYTHING NICE— SHUT UP

A really easy rule to understand but a tough one to follow. We all like to gossip, to bitch, to talk about our boss behind their back. The rule, however, is – don't do it. Learn to say only positive things, nice things, complimentary things. People judge you by what you say as much as how you say it (*see Part 2*), so be known as someone who is always pleasant and upbeat.

RULE 31

Don't Gossip

"Did you know that at the last company conference Steve, from accounts was seen coming out of Debbie's, from marketing, bedroom in the early hours of Sunday morning? And that twice since they have been seen in Luigi's at lunchtime and Kathy swears she's seen them holding hands in the elevator. Steve's married, you know, and I thought Debbie was engaged. What do you think? Should they be carrying on like this?"

Answer: "What's this got to do with me?"

Good, it has nothing to do with you, unless Steve happens to be your boss and his work is being affected, or you happen to be Debbie's fiancé. This rule says that you don't gossip. It doesn't say you don't listen. You may find it interesting and knowing what's going on comes in useful sometimes. But there is one part of this rule which is really, really simple— don't pass anything on. That's it. Gossip stops with you. If you listen but don't pass it along or offer an opinion you'll be seen as "one of us" rather than a party pooper. You don't have to be seen disapproving—merely don't pass anything along.

Gossiping is the occupation of idle minds—those who haven't got enough work to do. It is also the domain of workers who have mindless jobs to do—jobs they can do without thinking and thus have to occupy themselves with inane chatter, tittle tattle, rumor, lies, and malicious stories. Trouble is that if you

> ## "THERE IS ONE PART OF THIS RULE WHICH IS REALLY, REALLY SIMPLE— DON'T PASS ANYTHING ON."

don't join in you can be seen as severe or stuck up. You have to look as if you gossip without ever doing it. Don't go getting all hoity-toity and telling everyone how silly they are doing it.

With most things discretion is the key word. Don't be seen disapproving—just don't do it and keep that to yourself.

Don't Bitch

Yep, life ain't fair. Sometimes colleagues shirk and you end up with extra work; bosses can be ill prepared for their jobs and as such are incompetent and often inconsistent; idiots get promoted all around you; there's too much work to do; there are too many stupid systems in place; idiots thwart you at every turn. It's true, life's a bitch.

Now tell me how moaning helps in any one of these scenarios. Tell me how moaning will change one single thing. It won't. It doesn't. Moaning is a time-wasting device invented by sad people who haven't enough work to do. And they're usually the ones standing next to the ones gossiping. They may even be the same ones—chances are they are. And when they've finished having a good moan, they'll have a good gossip.

Moaning is pointless. It is unproductive and achieves nothing. All it does is:

- Identifies you as idle, petty, trivial
- Encourages you to turn the corners of your mouth down—not attractive
- Wastes time
- Makes you a magnet for other moaners
- Gets you a reputation as someone who doesn't offer anything productive or helpful
- Demotivates you and sets up a vicious circle

So, what are you going to do if you are a habitual moaner? Easy, make sure that whenever you do moan you make yourself offer a solution to whatever it is you are moaning about. If you can't see a solution you aren't allowed to moan. Try that for a few weeks and you'll stop moaning quite naturally.

Bitching about others invariably takes place behind their backs. Next time you feel the need for a good bitch about someone make yourself go and do it to their face. If they aren't present in the room, don't do it. Simple rule but it works. Once they are there you'll stop bitching, it's too hard to keep doing it when you've upset everyone in the office. If you've got something to say, say it to their face (but do see the introduction to this rule first—*If you can't say anything nice—shut up*).

> ## "MOANING IS POINTLESS. IT IS UNPRODUCTIVE AND ACHIEVES NOTHING."

RULE 33

Stand Up for Others

So, you're all sitting around having coffee when the subject of young Adam comes up. Now we all know that Adam is a pain in the backside. He doesn't pull his weight, arrives late and leaves early, steals the pens and paperclips, is rude to the security staff, always offloads as much work onto others as possible, blames others for his mistakes, and is generally obnoxious. So you all have a moan about him behind his back and get a lot of your anger about his behavior off your chest. But *you* don't. Oh, the others might but you won't, not from now on. You are now a Rules Player and you stand up for others.

No matter how obnoxious young Adam is you will always find something nice—and genuine—to say about him. That is your objective—*find something nice to say no matter what.*

At first this may be quite hard but if you persevere it becomes increasingly easy—it's all a question of habit and mental outlook. If we are used to bitching and moaning then that's what we do. But if we change our approach we can be more positive—but it does take a bit of effort initially to make this change.

Standing up for others, no matter what, gets you a reputation as someone who can always find something nice to say about everybody. Thus, those who you would have moaned about know that you, of all the work force, will always be fighting their corner for them. It gets you unwritten loyalty and a sort of guardian angel relationship with the more unpopular members of the team.

This is a strange relationship to have but it works wonders— these are the people who will back you in an emergency. They will let you know if someone is trying to set you up. They will pull out all the stops for you because they know you care. If you need a favor they will be the ones to call on.

It's amazing how quickly the word will spread that you are a thoroughly nice person—you don't bitch, you don't moan, you stand up for the underdog, you are supportive and can always see at least one good point in a thoroughly bad apple.

Obviously you will have to do this in an honest and sincere fashion—it's no good lying or making it up. If you, at first, simply can't find anything positive to say then shut up. But there is always something nice to say—nobody is completely evil or wicked or nasty.

So, back to young Adam. What are you going to say? Well, for a start you could point out that he makes good coffee. Or that he is always on time. Or he is very good at handling irate customers. Or he has a brilliant sense of humor. Or he always knows the football scores. Just keep saying "But he's good because he ...."

RULE 34

Compliment People Sincerely

The key to this rule is "sincerely." You mustn't use compliments glibly, falsely, shallowly, dishonestly, or disingenuously. Compliments must be real, honest, open, guileless, and meaningful.

Being the sort of person who gives compliments is quite tricky. You don't want to be seen as a slimeball or spooky—and people who do give compliments can often end up seen like this—but you do want to come over as genuinely warm and friendly.

So how to do this? And why? Well, if you do it affably it makes people think incredibly well about you—it is good office karma. The best way to do it is by being unsophisticated about it. All you have to do is say "I really like the way you've had your hair cut," and then ask a question about whatever it is you are complimenting them on, and make it about *how* it was done. "So who did your hair?"

"I do like the way you handled that customer, how did you feel saying that?"

"I must say I liked your report, how is it going down with the board?"

Try to avoid using hyperbole. You don't "love" their new coat, you merely "like" it. Remember if you "love" it, you'll want to marry it and have its babies. Not true of a coat, or a report, or a hairstyle, or the way someone handles a customer.

If you "like" something, feel free to say so. You can emphasize how much you like something by:

- "I really like ...."
- "I do like ...."
- "Can I tell you how much I liked ...."

And it doesn't just have to be "liked," although it is a very good one to start with:

- "I was impressed by ...."
- "I thought you did really well ...."
- "The way you did ... was very good indeed."
- "I did enjoy your presentation. It was really rather exceptional."

When giving compliments make sure you can't be accused of flirting or coming on to someone—keep it professional and/or work related. I'm sure you don't need telling this.

Be Cheerful and Positive

If you go into work each morning with a positive vibe it sets you up as the sort of person to whom stress and troubles and problems are but as water off a duck's back. You thus get a reputation as being someone who is in control, smooth, relaxed, confident, and very mature. And all for the sake of a few bars of Moon River, whistled as you make your way to your desk.

Be cheerful at all times. So it's raining out there and it's a dark and depressing winter's afternoon. Business is slack, interest rates have just gone up again, and the boss is in a foul mood and everyone's keeping their heads down. It's still no reason to lose your smile. So it's a bad day, this too will pass and the sun will come back. Whatever your situation things will always get better.

Maintaining a cheerful and positive outlook is a trick. At first you don't have to believe it—just do it. Act it. Pretend. But do it. After a little while you'll find it isn't an act, you're not pretending, you genuinely do feel cheerful. It's a trick. You are tricking yourself, no one else. Putting on a smile triggers hormones. These hormones will make you feel better. Once you feel better you will smile more and thus produce more hormones. All it takes is the first few days smiling when you don't feel like it and you will start a cycle going that will make you feel better all the time.

Once you are seen as someone cheerful and positive, people will want to hang out with you more—there is nothing so attractive as a cheerful person.

Bring some flowers into work and brighten up your desk. Whistle. Smile. Laugh. Never reveal that you feel like the pits inside. It's all too easy when someone says "How are you?" to reply "Oh, OK, I guess, can't complain, mustn't grumble, you know, struggling on." It's a cliché. It's a habit. Try instead "Fine, really good actually, doing OK." There's a trick for you.

So someone brings you more work that you simply have to do—it's unavoidable and part of your remit, and just when you thought you could see a little light at the end of the tunnel. Easy to say "Oh no, not more damn work. Can't everybody see how busy I am? This really is too much." If it's unavoidable and moaning isn't going to change a thing then maybe saying, "Fine just dump it there, I'll get on with it in a moment. Thanks." Why berate the messenger. I'm sure they didn't personally generate all this extra work just to piss you off. So it's a drag having extra work to do. So what? So be cheerful and get on with it. Every second spent moaning and bitching is a second taken off your life. Every second spent being cheerful and positive is a second added on. Take your choice.

Ask Questions

The object of the exercise is to become:

- Popular
- Promotable
- Successful
- Thoroughly nice
- Efficient

One of the easiest ways to do this is to learn and practice the habit of asking questions. What sort of questions? Well, that depends, obviously on the situation. For instance in *Rule 34: Compliment people sincerely*, we used a couple of examples where the follow-up question is useful—"I really liked your presentation. I thought you were incredibly calm. How do you avoid shaking?" Or—"I like your new method of handling invoices. What gave you the idea?"

Asking questions shows that you have paid attention, care, are interested, are thoughtful, are considerate and intelligent and creative. Stupid people don't ask questions. Bored people don't ask questions. Lazy people don't ask questions. Any questions?

Belligerent people tend to make statements—"I don't like that idea, it's unworkable." Rules Players ask questions; they might mean the same thing but they handle it differently—"I think I need more information about this idea. How do you see it working? Will dispatch be able to handle the increase in orders? Can we provide enough extra staff to cover? Maybe we all need to go away and think about this one, what does everyone else think?" You haven't said the idea stinks but they know you think that, but they also think you're a thoroughly nice person—you haven't shot them down in flames in front of their colleagues, but you have given them enough rope to hang themselves if they want to. And you've given them a get out if they choose to take it—go away and think about it a bit more means let's not hear about this again, but it's a very diplomatic way of saying so.

Asking questions is a very nice thing to do in a general way. It shows you are interested in your colleagues. But do make the questions genuine and sincere, worthwhile, and kind.

There's very little point is asking: "Where on earth did you get that coat? You can't think it suits you, surely?" Much better not to dwell on the coat if it really is horrible. Ask instead about the work: "How come you can always do this invoicing so quickly? Do you have some secret the rest of us don't have?"

As in the case of standing up for someone—even if they are loathsome there will always be some good point about them, no one is totally wicked—so too with questions. There will always be some aspect of someone's work that you could ask about or their hobbies or social life or family. Even if it's a simple: "How are the kids?" it cuts the ice and makes you nice. It opens up dialogue, generates pleasantness, and creates warmth among people who have to work together every day.

Use "Please" and "Thank You"

You would have thought this one so obvious, so basic and so fundamental that surely it can't be part of the Rules. Sorry, but we all need reminding that saying "please" and "thank you" is very important. It just doesn't happen enough. People say that they are too busy or too forgetful, or that it should be taken as read that they have said them and they don't need to each and every time. Rubbish. The only reason please and thank you get forgotten is plain old bad manners. If we start ignoring even the basic levels of human decency and politeness then there really is no point to any of us being here. If we aren't civil and civilized enough to thank someone, or to be bothered enough to say please, then it really is time to pack it in.

It doesn't matter how many times a day someone passes you a piece of paper—it is "thank you" every single time without fail or exception. It doesn't matter how many times you have to ask for the same thing—you always say "please." If someone does anything for you, no matter how mundane, trivial, repetitive, boring, effortless, you will always say thank you.

You forget one time and you will be labeled as rude, boorish, and unpleasant. Make someone's day and don't forget, please. Thank you. I once worked with a manager who could get staff to work the graveyard shift, come in during their vacations, work overtime, work their days off, take work home with them, work at weekends and work harder than any other manager could. We all watched him, trying to work out what it was he was doing that we weren't. He was getting loyalty from his team that we weren't. I know you are ahead of me at this stage and have got your hand up with the answer. He said "please" and "thank you."

Yes, happy now? He did indeed. And that simple bit of politeness went a long way. I don't think his staff consciously knew he did it. We certainly couldn't spot it for a long time. Most of us reckoned we also said "please" and "thank you." But he said it without fail every single time. And when you say it, mean it. A sincere and warm thank you goes a long way. It is also a very good way to respond to compliments and praise yourself. If someone says you have done something well, don't blush and stammer "It was nothing really." That subtracts from their compliment. Better instead just to say, "Thank you." Never use the word please to wheedle or cajole. It is "Could you work through this lunchtime, please, as we need extra cover on the phones and I'll make sure you get the time back a bit later this afternoon." It is not *Pleeeeease* can you work, pretty *pleeeease*."

Don't Curse

I know we all do it. I know you think it's cool. I know we have to be modern and move with the times. But I'm sorry, cursing isn't allowed. You can say what you want when you get home, or in the car on your own. But at work you don't curse. It's a simple rule but it works because it is a default setting—you don't curse. Now what decisions and choices do you have to make about that? Answer: None. None whatsoever. It is your bottom line. You don't curse, so all the tricky stuff has been taken away from you.

But if cursing is your default setting, you have so many decisions and choices to make, I'm surprised you get any work done at all. For instance do you:

- Curse every time something goes wrong?
- Curse over the phone?
- Curse in front of the boss?
- Curse in front of customers?
- Curse at customers?
- Limit yourself to certain curse words and not use others?
- Use religious blasphemy as curse words?
- Limit yourself to mild cursing or go for the really offensive?

> ## "YOU CAN SAY WHAT YOU WANT WHEN YOU GET HOME, OR IN THE CAR ON YOUR OWN. BUT AT WORK YOU DON'T CURSE."

It's a minefield. It's a nightmare. It really is so much easier to just not bother. This isn't a puritan dictate. It is an efficiency dictate. It saves time and effort and having to think about it if you simply don't do it. Now go away.

Be a Good Listener

I don't mean you should provide a nice padded shoulder for all and sundry to come and cry on. In fact that probably isn't good listening but therapy. A good listener is someone who makes the speaker know that they are listening. You do this by:

- Making encouraging noises—Hmmm, go on, yes, I'm listening.

- Displaying appropriate body language—Head tilted to one side, eyes open and looking at the person speaking, not yawning or fiddling with your watch.

- Repeating back some bits to make sure they know you've taken them in—On Friday at 3, yes, I've got that.

- Getting them to repeat things you haven't heard or understood—Can you repeat that bit about Minneapolis, I'm not sure I was taking that in?

- Asking questions—So the move to Seattle will not happen now?

- Taking notes—Write stuff down as they speak.

Now why would you want to be a good listener? I said, now why would you want to be a good listener? Easy. You get:

- More facts

- A better understanding of what you are supposed to be doing

- A better grasp of what is going on around you
- Seen as sympathetic and considerate
- Seen as intelligent and alert
- Seen as someone on top of their job

If you don't listen you don't know. If you are going to listen make sure they know you are. Easy.

Good listening is a skill, a special talent, that you will have to practice and learn. It doesn't happen overnight and it isn't automatic. You have to think about it and catch yourself when you aren't listening and turn it on then.

> "GOOD LISTENING IS A SKILL, A SPECIAL TALENT, THAT YOU WILL HAVE TO PRACTICE AND LEARN."

Only Speak Sense

To become successful and get promoted you have to project the right image—the wise, mature, reliable, cool, sophisticated, trustworthy, experienced business person—and there are times when all the hard work can be devastated, destroyed, by a careless word or unguarded moment. Recently, a government official was fired because she told a "racist" joke at a private function. Her career was brought down by an unguarded moment of not "speaking sense."

You have to guard your tongue against:

- Un-PC comments
- Offensive jokes or remarks that alienate any section of the community
- Sexism in any form
- Patronizing people
- Arrogance
- Loss of temper
- Offensive swearing—*see Rule 38*
- Bitching, moaning, gossiping—*see Rules 31–33*
- Revealing what you really think of people

It might be wise to learn to speak only occasionally, rather than blabbing on. If you let your tongue run away with itself,

> "THERE ARE TIMES WHEN ALL THE HARD WORK CAN BE DEVASTATED, DESTROYED, BY A CARELESS WORD OR UNGUARDED MOMENT."

it is so much more likely that you'll say the wrong thing. If you think carefully before you speak, pause and have a chance to bite your tongue then the chances are that your delivery will be accurate, your speech edited carefully and you will only speak sense. You thus get a reputation for being wise and mature. People will come to you for advice and guidance because they know you think about what you are going to say and don't just chatter on. They will trust you. Once trusted you are a natural candidate for promotion and success.

Make sure that what you have to say has an impact and isn't lost in the general hubbub of office clamor. Don't chat about what you watched on TV last night—to be honest no one is really interested—instead be silent until you have something important to offer.

PART 5

LOOK AFTER YOURSELF

Most people you deal with are probably decent and good to be around. However, there are always a few who aren't. You can't avoid them—the bastards, the jealous colleagues, the ones who will take any opportunity to stab you in the back or sabotage you. They'll shoot you down in flames at any chance they get. Make sure that your new image doesn't make you a target. This rule is about minimizing enemies and staying one jump ahead. As you get more successful it is often a sort of organic process that you attract jealousy and envy. By practicing this rule you will avoid this and look after yourself—especially your back.

RULE 41

Know the Ethics of Your Industry

So, what do you do for a living? I don't mean the actual job. I mean what contribution do you make to society? Is your contribution positive, beneficial, healthy? Or is it detrimental, negative, damaging? What does your industry do? How much a part of that industry are you? Have you considered the ethics of your industry?

What do we mean by ethics? Ethics are the morals of your industry—the rights and wrongs, the good and bad. Is your industry a good thing or a bad thing? Does it hurt or heal? Is it putting something positive into society or merely taking something out?

No, you don't have to walk out if you have just suddenly decided that your own particular industry stinks. What you can do is work from the inside to change things. I don't think we're talking environmental issues here, although I am aware that they may be of concern to a lot of us. Instead, I want you to concentrate on what your industry does morally.

Obviously, if you do decide that your industry is unjustified in its approach—and this happened to me and I walked—and you simply cannot live with it, then you have to get out. This is good karma and you gain benefit even if you do lose out financially.

Within your industry there will be good bits and bad bits. Occasionally, you will be asked to cross the line and do bad things. Obviously, you will have read *Rule 43: Set Personal Standards* but this is about helping set standards for your industry rather than personal ones. You have to point out that morally, ethically, what you are being asked to do is bad for the company. Constantly say, "What would the press do if they got hold of this?" and offer them a suitable headline: "Scrooge Ltd replaces sacked workers with Asian sweatshop labor."

Yes, you can be as assertive as you like and refuse, but you might just get labeled then as a wimp who is frightened to get their hands dirty—no guts, that sort of thing. No, you have to point out the ramifications for the company. You have to implant the idea of the whistleblower—"Hey what would they do with this?" This way you will be one of the company people while still playing the ethics card. You will be one of us and one of them all at the same time.

To do all this, you have to know the ethics of your industry and know what its contribution is. Do your research now.

Know the Legalities of Your Industry

Is your company breaking any laws? Are you breaking any laws? Do you know the legalities of your industry?

I once worked for an organization who were, initially, remarkably above board. They prided themselves on being a standard setter, a new thing in the industry. After a few years, they suddenly changed direction and lost the Jekyll to gain the Hyde. It was quite bizarre and I couldn't see why it happened. Senior board members hadn't changed that much and circumstances didn't seem to demand it—we weren't fighting for our lives here. But suddenly laws were being broken—and I do mean laws. Suddenly I found myself working for a crooked and corrupt company. What to do? I turned a blind eye for a while, but eventually I too was asked to participate in the law breaking. It was at that point I left. I kept my honor and reputation and went to work for the opposition, their rivals. Once there, I was asked about my old company and what it got up to, but I wouldn't give any information that would allow my new bosses to gain benefit over my old company. I don't know why, but it seemed honorable to sit on what I knew. I was happy to talk about the way they did business, just so long as it didn't spill over into this area of legalities.

A few years later I found myself working for a company that was taken over by my old corrupt bunch. By now they had been caught, punished and cleaned up their act. Did I want to work for them again? Not particularly. But I did have an interview with a senior director who said he was happy to have me on board—"At least you know how to keep your mouth shut," he said. The leopard still seemed a bit spotty to me and I walked.

So, how clean is your industry? Your company? You have to know what you might be asked to do and what is legal and what isn't. Some industries have incredibly minute and trivial laws that you can run foul of almost without realizing it. But realize it you must. To be a Rules Player you have to be cleaner than clean, above suspicion and never allow yourself to be scapegoated into anything. If they are looking for a sucker make sure it ain't you. Make sure you stay clearly this side of the line and don't stray over it accidentally.

If you choose to break the law that's one thing, but how awful it would be if you ended up in clink because you didn't know. Better to be an intelligent convict than a stupid one—"But I didn't know," has never been an effective defense.

Set Personal Standards

Do you sleep nights? I know I do, but then I set personal standards that I simply won't break.

- I will not knowingly hurt or hinder another human being in the pursuit of my career.

- I will not knowingly break any laws in the furtherance of my career.

- I will have a moral code that I will follow no matter what.

- I will endeavor to provide a positive contribution to society by what I do for a living.

- I will not do anything that I would be ashamed to talk to my children about.

- I will put my family first at all times.

- I will not work evenings or weekends, unless it is an emergency and I have discussed it with my partner.

- I will not unfairly stitch up anyone in my pursuit of new work.

- I will always endeavor to put something back.

- I will pass on freely and openly any skills, knowledge or experience to anyone who could use them to benefit themselves within the same industry—I won't hog information for the sake of it.

- I will not be jealous of anyone else's success in the same industry.
- I will question the long-term ramifications of what I do constantly.
- I will play by the Rules at all times.

This code of conduct is my own personal set of standards. It might not suit you. You may need or have a better set. I do hope you don't opt for a worse one. We must endeavor to be the very, very best we can at all times.

> "WE MUST ENDEAVOR TO BE THE VERY, VERY BEST WE CAN AT ALL TIMES."

Never Lie

This Rule, as in the case of *Rule 38: Don't Curse*, is very easy. It sets a limit which you don't have to think about. Never lie means exactly that—never lie. Under no circumstances do you lie. Once you have got a reputation as someone who never lies you won't ever be asked to cover up, or cover for anyone else.

If you do decide to lie for a living you have too many choices and decisions. Where do you draw the line? Do you only tell little lies? Great big ones? Do you lie to save yourself? Others? Do you lie for the company? For your boss? For colleagues? How developed will your lies be? Will you add lie to lie when the first lie looks like it's about to be detected? Where will you stop this process? Will you involve other people in your lies? Or will you be a lone liar?

Can you see the problems? If you have a simple rule—never lie— you have a default setting that requires no thought, no choices, no decisions, no alternatives, no picking, no preferences.

Not ever lying also saves you from guilt, fear, recrimination, having to remember the lies, the risk of being punished or fired or embarrassed, ostracizing your colleagues, putting your family in jeopardy, running the risk of a criminal prosecution, and not sleeping nights.

Never lie is really the simplest, cleanest, most honest approach to your working life and career.

> ## "YOU ARE ALLOWED TO TALK UP YOUR QUALITIES OR SKILLS OR EXPERTISE—JUST DON'T ACTUALLY TELL A LIE."

It is, of course, OK to embellish and hype up your resumé or experience or enthusiasm but please don't actually lie—you will be found out I guarantee it.

If I'm offering a book to a publisher and they ask me what it is like I don't say, "It's alright I suppose." No, instead I say, "It's brilliant, simply brilliant. It will sell extremely well and might well be the bestseller we're looking for." Is any of this a lie? Not really. I wouldn't be writing it if I didn't think it was brilliant. Will it sell that well? It might. Who am I to know for certain? It's a changeable market. Is it a lie to say it will? No.

You are allowed to talk up your qualities or skills or expertise—just don't actually tell a lie. And a lie is anything that can be proved definitely to be wrong. To say you are *qualified* as a software programmer when you aren't is a lie. To say you are a wizard at software programming isn't because it is a matter of opinion rather than fact. But if in doubt—never lie or embellish if you can't think fast on your feet.

Never Cover Up for Anyone Else

Being a Rules Player means you are aiming for perfection, that you are setting extremely high standards for yourself. Others will not have these standards—obviously they won't be as successful as you because of this—but they may well try to either get you to lower yours or to involve you in their shenanigans. What do you do? Again be happy with a simple default setting—you don't cover up for anyone, ever, under any circumstances.

This way it is simple. You don't have to think about this. You have no choices or decisions to make. You know exactly where you stand. You have let your colleagues know exactly where they stand. You have let your boss know that you won't cover for anyone, therefore, you are above suspicion, trustworthy, reliable, beyond reproach.

If you do decide to cover for others it complicates your life so much that it can't really be worth it. For instance, do you only cover for close colleagues or anyone who asks? Do you only cover for small incidents or the big ones? What about covering for fraud? Criminal negligence? What do you say and do when you get found out? How do you explain it to your family when you get fired?

How do you handle it when asked to cover up for a close colleague who might well be a friend as well? You can be fairly assertive and just say "No"—you don't have to explain. Or you can soften the blow by saying "Please don't ask me, I would have to say no if you do," to give them a get-out clause and save their face.

Once you have done this, it gets easier once you've established a reputation for not covering up. The hardest bit is ignoring the emotional blackmail that often accompanies a request to cover up for someone. But in reality that is quite easy to ignore in the sense that if they think so little of you to use this technique, then why the hell shouldn't you turn them down? They have already cooked their goose by using such an approach on you.

If they put pressure on you, adopt the stuck record technique and just keep saying "No, I can't, please don't ask. No, I can't, please don't ask …." They'll crack before you. Always remember that a real friend will never ask you to cover up for them.

Keep Records

When a publisher and I agree to do a book together we draw up a contract. This specifies all those things that could get forgotten along the way. That way, when I deliver the manuscript and the publisher says, "But this is only 100 pages and I thought we had agreed on 200," I can produce the contract and find the clause where it clearly states 100 pages, or so many words, or whatever.

If your boss asks you to do something and you make a note of it—in front of them—they have a very hard job arguing later that you've done it wrong or late.

If you have to submit a report then drop your boss a quick memo or note outlining the salient facts, very briefly, so there will be no confusion later. Keep a copy. Make sure they know you have kept a copy.

This technique isn't to cover your back because you are up to no good. Instead it clarifies all issues. If it's in writing it makes your job so much simpler, so much easier. Who can argue with a written memo? In fact such things could be forged, written afterward, changed, amended, and/or rewritten but we all assume they aren't, that they are tamper proof.

It is amazing how often the tiniest detail will cause a major upset—unless you got it in writing in the first place. Keeping records isn't an anal thing to do, but a sensible precaution. None of us has perfect memory. We all forget things—dates, times, details. Once we have made a note of whatever it is we can refer to it later. And often surprise ourselves with how badly we have remembered something.

You will often read in management books the advice to throw away all memo or emails or faxes over a certain age—if you haven't looked at it in six months then you don't need it. Rubbish. You hang on to everything. Make more filing space rather than throw anything away, unless and until you are 100 percent certain it is not needed. I once had a major row with a publisher (not this one, of course) relating to a book I had written for them five years previously. It was a dispute that wasn't covered by anything in the contract. But I had kept my original notes and could produce them—bit like having to show your workings during maths at school—but I still had my workings and could show that what they had published had been exactly what they had asked for. I was off the hook. You won't get me throwing anything away. No way.

Know the Difference Between the Truth and the Whole Truth

Although we have ascertained that you ain't never ever gonna lie and you don't cover up for colleagues no matter what, you don't have to be a goody goody and tell tales. You don't need to volunteer information unless it directly helps you to do so. Knowing that a colleague has messed up doesn't mean you have to run to the boss and rat on them. Instead, it might be beneficial sometimes to stand back and watch how things develop. If your colleague knows you know and you ain't saying anything, there might be a favor being born there that could be recalled later.

And, of course, if you do get asked, you don't lie. But again know the difference between the truth and the whole truth. Not lying is one thing, throwing up and regurgitating everything you do know is something else. Sometimes it pays to be a little editorial with what truth you are giving out. The beauty of being a Rules Player is that you get on and are successful and you are still able to live with yourself—to be a thoroughly nice person. This means you don't lie and don't cover up, but it also means you don't spy on your colleagues, rat on them, betray them, get them involved unnecessarily.

Look, it's a real world out there and it can be dog eat dog. Be careful, there are some pretty unsavory characters. There may be ruthlessness going on around you, but you don't have to participate. You don't have to be a teacher's pet either. Keep your wits about you at all times and know when to spill the beans and when to shut the duck up.

I guess you have to be a diplomat—knowing what to say and when to say it; martial arts expert—thinking on your feet; therapist—letting others bring their problems to you, but you keep yours to yourself; and Zen master—all-seeing, all-knowing, saying little.

So when someone asks for your opinion you have to weigh up what it is they are really asking. Do they really want the truth? Their report sucks. Or a limited version of the truth? Your report is fine, it'll just about do the job. A highlighted truth? Your report is good but you have missed out quite a lot. A reassurance truth? Your report is really good and I liked it, and I like you because your report is so good. Or the real truth? I haven't had time to read it yet because I don't like you and think it'll be a pretty boring report—bit like you really.

RULE 48

Cultivate Your Support/Contacts/ Friends

If you don't cover up for people, what use are you to them? As I have said it's a real world out there and people expect a lot of you. They want you to be in their debt. They want you to carry the can, cover up for them, do their dirty work for them and watch their back—and all at the same time. But you are a Rules Player now and that takes you outside the spheres of petty office gang warfare. You are now a stand-alone item. You don't feed with the sharks and yet you avoid being their food. What are you and what are you for?

You are a pool of calm, the eye of the storm. You are the reliable strength of the team, unshakeable and unshaken. You are the default setting, the honesty factor, the standard by which all other colleagues judge themselves. If you think it's a no-go area then they will know it is. If you turn your back on a tricky situation they too will know it's not to be touched. If you say it's fine, then they know it's a good thing.

You are the standard bearer, the criteria by which all else is judged. Don't believe me? Try it, it works.

And because you are so reliable, honest, trustworthy other colleagues will quickly come to rely on you for advice and guidance. You, however, give nothing away for free. Every pat on the back, every prod in the right direction, every session of useful hints and tips, every point of guidance comes with a price—loyalty. You may not hunt with the pack, but by golly the pack had better know who really is pack leader. Yep, you. How to achieve this? By kindness, by consideration, by playing it straight. Never let them down. Never rat on them. Never drop them in it. Always be cheerful, supportive, loyal— don't lie or cover up, but do close ranks if you can—protective, cooperative, caring and genuinely interested in them as human beings. You'll have 'em eating out of your hand. Why? Because this is a rare game to play. Playing it straight is such an unusual thing that they will have no defense against it, no protection. There are few management training books or courses that teach you to be nice, be straight, be honest. The unspoken wisdom is generally be ruthless, take advantage, dog eat dog. The consequence of this is everyone thinks like a dog and not like a real person. You come along and show them how it really should be and they will follow you anywhere, you old dog you.

RULE 49

Understand Others' Motives

So what motivates you? We know that you are a Rules Player—honest, diligent, hardworking, keen, successful and self-motivated. You get off on doing a job fabulously well, impressing your bosses, earning the respect of your colleagues and the admiration and loyalty of your juniors. You go home at night knowing you've done a good day's work and that you've been pleasant to everyone and are a thoroughly nice person. You sleep nights because you haven't aggravated anyone or broken any laws or behaved badly in any way. You earn lots, but that isn't your driving force—yours is the need to be the very best, the finest that there is. But what motivates them? Ah, to really get on you will need to understand the motives of others.

Understanding their motives means you have to enter the dark and nebulous world of psychology. What gets others off can be very diverse:

- Power
- Money
- Prestige
- Revenge
- A need to hurt
- A need to be loved.

Whatever their motives I can bet they aren't Rules Players—you lot stand out a mile—aloof, calm, in control, dignified, and sophisticated. Anybody whose motives are need and fear and greed should be treated carefully. You will have to make sure you stay on the right side of them without fawning, that you outmaneuver them without sinking to their level and without being paranoid. Look around your office now and identify what makes each of your colleagues tick, and do the same for your boss and their boss. Learn to identify their motives and you will be able to handle them easily. Knowledge is power.

> "ANYBODY WHOSE MOTIVES ARE NEED AND FEAR AND GREED SHOULD BE TREATED CAREFULLY."

RULE 50

Assume Everyone Else Is Playing by Different Rules

So we know what rules you are following, but what about other people? What are their standards? What rule book are they following, what drum beat do they march to? Chances are they are making it up as they go along. This makes them unpredictable and erratic.

Not everybody will have your high standards of honesty and morality. Obviously, some people are kind and dignified—just like you—and are still able to climb the corporate ladder. But there are equally lots out there whose rules are suspect.

The rule book you now have must remain a secret. If you reveal your rules you have broken the rules. If you assume that everyone else is playing by different rules you won't go far wrong. You don't have to assume that their rules are better or worse than yours, merely different. If you assume that their rules are the same as yours or better you will be constantly let down, disappointed, disillusioned, saddened, and upset.

> "THE RULE BOOK
> YOU NOW HAVE
> MUST REMAIN
> A SECRET.
> IF YOU REVEAL
> YOUR RULES YOU
> HAVE BROKEN
> THE RULES."

If you assume their rules are worse than yours you will grow mistrustful, apprehensive, paranoid, suspicious, and sceptical.

Assuming that their rules are different without assuming what those rules are keeps you open and receptive, cautious but expectant, approachable but not overly trustful, responsive but not gullible.

It's a bit like being a martial arts exponent:

- You are alert and prepared, but not muscle bound or aggressive.
- You remain flexible and fluid and can move like a cat and dodge whatever is thrown your way without ever adopting a belligerent stance.
- You are ready for anything by being grounded and centered.

BLEND IN

No one likes a black sheep or a white crow or a fish that swims in a different direction to the rest of the shoal. Part 6 teaches you how to blend in, become "one of them" so you don't stand out as an outsider. You might stand out as being the leader of the pack—better, more efficient—but you'll still be "one of us" because you know how to play the "blending in" game.

Know the Corporate Culture

Every corporation, company, industry, or even small office has a culture. Knowing what that culture is gives you the edge, the key to success. Knowledge is power.

The culture is how their people do things. This culture is sometimes company led, but mostly people generated—it grows organically and without plan or strategy. If you don't know this culture—or fail to make use of it—you can end up looking foolish and are then easy to take advantage of, or be belittled.

Bear in mind that around 70 percent of all dismissals are not because someone couldn't do their job properly, but because they didn't know the corporate culture—they didn't fit in.

Consider this advert for a pretty big prestigious design studio—the BMD. When Bruce Mau, the owner of this company, wanted to recruit new staff, he put out a quiz with some 40 questions, including, "Who made a film consisting of nothing but the color blue?"*

* By the way it was Derek Jarman of course.

> # "YOU DON'T HAVE TO BUY INTO THE CORPORATE CULTURE —YOU DON'T HAVE TO BELIEVE IN IT— ALL YOU HAVE TO DO IS FIT IN."

Bruce headed the advert, "Avoid fields. Jump fences." As a result of this, he lured some of the best, most talented top designers to come and work for him—or *with* him, as he describes his working relationship with his staff.

Now what sort of corporate culture do you think Bruce expects, wants, gets? How would you fit in? What do you think Bruce would expect of you?

You don't have to buy into the corporate culture—you don't have to believe in it—all you have to do is fit in. If they all play golf, then you play golf. I know you hate golf, but you will play golf—if that's what it takes to fit in. Now you may, of course, question whether you want to fit in. You may question whether playing golf is where you want to be. But if you are a Rules Player and you want to get on and be successful and you also want to be part of a particular company where playing golf is the corporate culture—then play it you must.

Speak the Language

Fitting in means being able to follow the corporate culture, and speaking the language is a big part of this. You can give the game away by not using the right jargon, or using computer-speak at the wrong time. If they all use geeky language, then you too must use it. No, this isn't the time or place to discuss whether you want to belong to a geeky company—that's for you to do alone in the soul searching time of the early hours when you can't sleep.

If the boss talks in terms of SPRs for staff/product/ratios then you too must talk of SPRs. It isn't your job to educate them, re-educate them, edify them, inform them, teach them, give them a bit of class, drag them up, stop the dumbing down process, or instruct them. Their corporate language is what you must speak. I know there will be times when it will make you want to scream—but speak it you must.

I once worked for an Italian boss who, because of his inadequate grasp of English had taken to talking of "clienters," which was his sort of mix of clients and customers. Because he was the boss, this ridiculous term had entered public domain and every member of staff from the general manager down talked about the clienters. I could have stood there and screamed "No, no, no, this is wrong, stop it at once." It wouldn't have done me any good. It was clienters the whole time I was there and I hated it every time I heard it. But I knew the Rules and also called them clienters.

Spend a little time listening to how your office uses language. Do they speak proper English or a curious local variation? We're not talking accents here, but the sort of individual clienters that every office somehow manages to pick up. I also worked with an American who talked of people working as hard as Mexicans. This was his way of being, what he thought, politically correct. It was, of course, just as bad, just as wrong, just as offensive. However, he was the owner of the company so the term "Mexicans" had stuck and again it was wrong and horrible, but it was in current usage.

The only time this rule should be broken is where it applies to swearing. The Rules say no cursing, but if the corporate culture is that everyone curses what are you to do? Answer: not curse. *Rule 3.8* over-rules *Rule 52* in this case—you've been trumped.

> ## "IF THEY ALL USE GEEKY LANGUAGE, THEN YOU TOO MUST USE IT."

RULE 53

Dress Up or Down Accordingly

We talked earlier about always dressing elegantly, stylishly, smartly but what if you go to work for that design company where they all wear jeans and a T-shirt? In your case, you will have to wear jeans too. Just make sure your jeans are the smartest, the most stylish, the most fashionable, the most modern—no, no, you do not iron them, no creases, for God's sake!

Watch what the others do. If, at a meeting, it is jackets off and sleeves rolled up then that's what you do. If it is very formal and jackets stay on, then yours stays on as well. I know this may sound obvious, but you would be surprised how often you look around a meeting and you can see the one person marching to a different drumbeat—and that's the one who will be ostracized by the others.

To a greater or lesser extent, we all need to belong to the herd, to fit in, to blend in, to camouflage ourselves so we don't draw unnecessary attention to ourselves. Obviously, if it is the boss who takes their jacket off then you too do so. Don't become a clone though and mindlessly follow what everyone else is doing. We are talking here of dressing up or down on a general basis not each and every minute.

I've always found it better to sit back for a moment or two to see what others do rather than to be the first to follow the head lemming. Stand back for a moment, it might be a cliff and not a promotion opportunity; or a springboard with no water below.

I've always found it useful to have a role model to check with to see if they would have done a certain thing, or worn a certain style of dress. For a lot of my business life I've used Cary Grant. Easy then to ask, "Would Cary have worn this?" If the answer is yes, then go right ahead. If the answer is no, then don't. See how easy this is. Try Humphrey Bogart, but in *Casablanca* rather than the *African Queen*.

Even if the corporate culture is to dress casual you can still make an effort.

RULE 54

Be Adaptable in Your Dealings with Different People

Being a chameleon is a good thing just so long as you can carry it off. People are all different and if you try to treat them all the same you run the risk of offending them all or at least failing to satisfy any of them.

It is a lot easier if you are a parent to understand this rule. If you have more than one child, you will know how essential it is *not* to treat them the same. Each child needs different motivating forces. For some it is enough to be mildly disappointed. For others you have to be a real ogre just to get them to get dressed in the morning.

I have five sons and a daughter and I have to treat each one differently. Sometimes I forget and treat them all the same and they are quite surprised and quite hurt. Each needs me to be something different, something unique for them, something special. As a manager you are a sort of parent to your people and must treat them as individuals.

I once staged a completely fake loss of temper to get my own way over a fairly trivial matter. The person for whose benefit the tantrum was put on was so shocked that I was given into immediately. Now there are quite a few bosses around for whom such behavior would have been intolerable and I would have been shown the door immediately.

When I was a general manager I always felt I could get the best out of my work force by being fairly pleasant and quite kind. But there were the odd few who didn't respond to this type of behavior. They were so entrenched in their old-fashioned approach to work that they expected a boss to be a complete bastard and to shout at them and tell them what to do. And here was me asking them how they were, and what they thought of it all. They couldn't cope and I had to be unpleasant to them to get them to respond—different strokes for different folks.

You have to be adaptable, ready to change quickly depending on what is required of you. The perfect manager is the one with the ability to spin on a dime. Study how you are with people. Are you always the same, no matter who they are or what is going on? Do you adapt and change readily and easily? Identify who around you is successful and watch what they do with people.

Know Where to Hang Out, and When

There are always key places where the high and mighty gather at formal and informal times. You need to check these places out and use them, as important places to garner information, make contacts, be seen and make an impact. Outside of work there will be a watering hole used by senior bosses. It might be the golf club 19th hole, the local bar, a certain restaurant, a club. Whatever, wherever. It is your duty to know where this is. Now don't go rushing in there and make a complete idiot of yourself. You have to spy out the land, reconnoitre the territory so as to be informed of everything you need to know before going in. Does the restaurant have a dress code or style you should know about? Is there a waiting list for membership of the golf club? Is the bar the sort of place you'd go alone or should you go with your partner? Is the club easy to join? Can you just hang out with the bosses without looking out of place? Are these places the sort you could just happen to be there, "I was just passing" or will it be obvious that you are hanging around waiting to make a move?

You have to be careful with this one, but you should know where they meet and the accessibility of such places. Chances

> # "GET YOUR FACE KNOWN, GET YOUR NAME KNOWN."

are you might choose never to go there. That's fine. But if it comes up in conversation you will have an edge just knowing where they go—knowledge is power.

In work there may be a corridor where they hang out next to the coffee machine or photocopier. You can always make sure you happen to be passing. Get your face known, get your name known.

At formal occasions perhaps the bosses all duck out for a smoke. Even if you don't indulge you can still pop out yourself and be part of that smoking gang. Or maybe they all like to visit the bar before going into the conference or whatever. Make sure you are there first so you don't have to have an excuse for dropping in.

RULE 56

Understand the Social Protocols

Within every company and place of work there will be social protocols. Know them and use them. They might be quite simple:

- You never take partners to the staff do.

- You always turn up for the staff meetings on your days off.

- You never park in a certain couple of spaces even though they aren't marked because they are unofficially reserved for the managing director's partner and kids.

- You never take the jelly doughnut with the coffee because that's Sylvia's—always has been, always will be.

- You always refer to the managing director as Charles to his face but as Charlie to the rest of the staff, but as Mr. Charles to his PA.

- It is OK to order wine with lunch but beer really is frowned on.

You may never know where some of these unwritten rules come from—Charles once got soundly thumped by a beer-drinking employee, hence no beer at lunch; Charles was once embarrassed by the wife of a junior manager who made a not completely unsuccessful pass at him at a staff do, hence no partners.

Of course, these social protocols may be obvious—Sylvia likes the jelly doughnuts and she has both the clout and juice to get her own way—the important thing is to identify them, file them away if you like but by golly you'd better know them if you don't want to make any terrible social gaffes.

I once worked for a company where it was considered taboo to drink during a working day in any way. You couldn't even have a beer at lunch. Alcohol was a big no, no and I couldn't find out why. I was happy to go along with this, as I am no drinker, but it puzzled me. I eventually found out that the company had had a finance manager who had spent every afternoon having forty winks in his office—sleeping it off. In fact he wasn't. He did drink a lot every lunchtime, but the afternoons were spent carefully siphoning off funds to his own accounts. He was eventually caught and dismissed, but after that no drinking was the rule—and no closed office doors.

"OF COURSE, THESE SOCIAL PROTOCOLS MAY BE OBVIOUS—THE IMPORTANT THING IS TO IDENTIFY THEM, FILE THEM AWAY."

RULE 57

Know the Rules About Authority

Who runs your office? I bet it ain't the boss. Bosses tend to closet themselves away in their ivory office, leaving the real job of running the business to someone else. Your job is to identify this person and stay on the right side of them.

I have worked for companies where the real power resided in the hands of a PR consultant, a legal secretary, an auditor, a customer and a junior manager. In each and every case, the reason why this particular person was really in charge was that they:

- Had the ear of the boss

- Were trusted by the boss

- Carried out a subtle whispering campaign rather than saying anything outright or up front

- Had been there quite some time

- Were motivated entirely by power and control

- Were invariably unpleasant enough to use various tactics to get their own way—no matter what

- Were extremely clever, but lacking the experience, qualifications, or skill to actually do the job properly.

In each case, once I had made a friend of these people I got on better. To begin with I didn't spot them immediately. This

> **"I HAVE WORKED FOR COMPANIES WHERE THE REAL POWER RESIDED IN THE HANDS OF A PR CONSULTANT, A LEGAL SECRETARY, AN AUDITOR, A CUSTOMER, AND A JUNIOR MANAGER."**

always caused me problems. I would go to the boss and only later be made to realize I had committed a gaffe by doing so— "Oh everything goes through Sarah first," "I'll just run it by Janine first to see if she thinks it a good idea," "Do you want to check this out with Trevor and come back to me?"

I soon learned to go to the person who had the ear of the boss first. Play the game with them and don't make an enemy of them. They are the real authority and you should pay them homage. I know it ain't fair and you hate it, but until a better system comes along we have to work with what we've got.

Know the Rules About the Office Hierarchy

This rule goes hand in hand with the previous one. You have to know who has the boss's ear and you have to know who runs the office. You might be quite senior but you won't get the key to the stationery cupboard no matter what, not unless you speak nicely to Mark first.

Office protocols and hierarchies are old fashioned, petty, small minded, outdated, and yet still very much with us. It wasn't that long ago that I worked in an office where you had to take your typing to an office manager who then handed it to a typist and it was returned to you later, all done.

Trouble was that if you upset the office manager—and you could do this by talking about the boss in a derogatory way, cursing, coming to work causally dressed—you got your work given to the worst typist and it came back late, full of mistakes, coffee cup stained, misspelled, no copies, you name it.

Once you got on the right side of the office manager, it all changed and your typist presented you with exemplary work, on time and immaculate.

Now you might say that this was the way it was and I couldn't really complain. Yes, but the office manager wasn't my office manager. I only used the typing facility occasionally and I was senior. I still had to go through this hierarchy which involved me in having to seek the patronage of someone junior to get a fairly mundane and routine job done. It sure made me mad and I had to spend quite a lot of time wooing the office manager just to get a letter done. It was time-consuming, unproductive, and petty. But you're right, we have to work with what we've got.

So what do we do? We play the game. We have no choice but to smile and woo them.

> "OFFICE PROTOCOLS AND HIERARCHIES ARE OLD FASHIONED, PETTY, SMALL MINDED, OUTDATED, AND YET STILL VERY MUCH WITH US."

Never Disapprove of Others

So, they're all going to the sports bar again this lunchtime. You hate that. You hate the smoke, the noise, the inane chatter about last night's TV.

But do you tell them this? No, you do not. You need to be one of the crowd—blend in. You need them to think you're there, in spirit if not in body, without actually being there. Easy. You get out of it by saying you have to do some shopping, visit a friend, go to the gym.

Don't disapprove of the way they spend their lunch break— this will make them think of you as an outsider. Nor do you tell them you're staying in the office to catch up on some work—they will think you a creep. But it is fine to say you are going to do some shopping and then find somewhere nice to park up in your car with a soft drink and a decent sandwich— and your laptop. You can get all that extra work done but you don't have to let them know.

Don't tell them that you think drinking at lunchtime is unhealthy and unproductive—tell them you'll be along in a bit and to carry on without you—"have one for me." This way the lunchtime crowd will accept you as "one of them" without you ever having to be one. You will be accepted if you don't disapprove.

Or perhaps they all go bowling together on a Tuesday evening. No, you don't say "but bowling is for geeks isn't it?" Instead you can say, "ah, Tuesday evenings? That's my night for taking my mother to the movies." Or how about you swallow your pride, your standards and your disapproval—and actually go. Who knows, maybe you'll have fun. But you will blend in and you won't show that you disapprove of your colleagues. Smart move.

How others spend their leisure time, their money or their lives is no concern of yours. The smart mover concentrates on their own path and ignores the route others choose to take. Keep focused on where you are going and ignore anything others are up to. By ignoring it is easier to stop making judgments. If you make judgments you categorize yourself and thus make it much more difficult to be flexible and to move easily from situation to situation. By judging others you, in turn, get pigeon-holed yourself—not a good place to be.

RULE 60

Understand the Herd Mentality

People like to form nice safe little groups—family, friends, work colleagues, town, country, nation, regiment—and will fight quite fiercely to protect these groups. If you threaten them—or, and this is important, are *thought* to threaten them—they won't like it. So don't. Understand that this herd mentality is important and that to blend in is important.

Suppose your herd is a pride of lions. Yes, you can roll in the dust, roar, eat zebras, and be very fierce and you will blend in—you will be a lion. This doesn't mean you have to capitulate though or be weak. In every pride there is a top dog—a senior lion. You can blend in but still stand out by being in charge, being a pack leader, being the head honcho.

Blending in is about being a chameleon not a wimp. Just because I say you ought to blend in doesn't mean you have to give up your identity or become a clone or lose all sense of your individuality. All you have to do is know and understand herd mentality—and then use it to your own advantage. I once saw an employee reduced to tears because he didn't know the system and the herd—his fellow workers—turned on him. He was "different" and they smelled his fear and went for him.

What you are going to be is the proverbial wolf in sheep's clothing. If the sheep accept you, then you can do pretty much

> ## "JUST BECAUSE I SAY YOU OUGHT TO BLEND IN DOESN'T MEAN YOU HAVE TO GIVE UP YOUR IDENTITY OR BECOME A CLONE OR LOSE ALL SENSE OF YOUR INDIVIDUALITY."

what you want with them. If they detect any whiff of wolfishness they start to get very unsettled.

Study any group of people and you will see conformity. They all like to be sheep, it makes them feel:

- Secure
- Comfortable
- Safe
- Protected

All their thinking has been done for them and they can just eat grass cosy and safe in the knowledge that they will be taken care of. You don't need these things, they're for the sheep. You are the wolf. Think independent, wolfish thoughts.

ACT ONE STEP AHEAD

If you are going to move on up you had better start practising now. Part 7 teaches you how to adopt the mannerisms, attitudes, and managerial traits of the position above the one you currently hold. If you already look as if you've been promoted, chances are you will be.

RULE 61

Dress One Step Ahead

When I was an assistant manager, I dressed like one. When I wanted to be a manager I studied what managers wore—and general managers. I opted to dress like a general manager and was duly promoted, thus missing out the manager's position in between assistant and general. There is a style for every job. You may choose what job you want. Now you can choose to dress like that job. Then you will get that job. It is that simple. Just so long as when you get that job you can do that job—don't fly until you can crawl.

I have held many interviews in my time for many different positions to be filled. I have never ceased to be amazed at how people dress for interviews. Is it like they don't want the job? I've seen interviews for senior management positions where the candidate has turned up in a crumbled suit, an unironed shirt or blouse, unpolished shoes and uncombed hair. I wouldn't employ them as—here I have to be careful as I don't want to insult any group of workers—ferret catchers.

I've seen interviews, again for senior management posts, where they turned up late, in the wrong place, on the wrong day, with the wrong information and obviously for the wrong job.

I've held interviews for trainees where they turned up in tennis shoes—not quite what I had in mind.

> ## "YOU MAY CHOOSE WHAT JOB YOU WANT. NOW YOU CAN CHOOSE TO DRESS LIKE THAT JOB. THEN YOU WILL GET THAT JOB."

Whatever job you are doing you must have your eye on the next position up. Haven't you? See *Part 3: Have a Plan*. If you have your eye on that job you must know who has that job now. Study them. What do they wear? How do they dress? What style, level of fashion? Is there anything you could learn from the way they dress? Can you start copying it now? And when I say copying it I do mean learning to dress like that for real. If it means wearing a smart business suit then get used to it.

There's nothing worse than starting a new job and starting to wear a new style at the same time. It will be noticed that the collar doesn't fit or the shoes seem too tight or strange, and that the level of fashion is all wrong for you—you're always pulling the hem of your skirt down or straightening that tie which feels so strange to you.

Talk One Step Ahead

How does your boss talk? I assume it is their job you want. If it ain't whose job is it? Or have I been wasting my time here? Come on, whose job do you want? Let's start with the boss. How does your boss talk?

What do I mean—how do they talk? I'll explain. It isn't their accent or pronunciation—how they sound—but the content, what they say. I bet you talk in terms of "I" whereas your boss will probably use "we" much more. You might speak from a worker's point of view, whereas they will speak on behalf of the company.

The more senior you go the less likely you are to:

- Chatter inanely.
- Gossip.
- Curse.
- Talk about last night's TV or any other issues that have no relevance to the work being done—bosses tend to be much more focused and less inclined to waste time.
- Babble on—bosses tend to be more thoughtful and pause before speaking (or at least the good ones do).

So if you are going to talk one step up, you need to be more thoughtful, talk about issues that are relevant, talk in terms of "we" rather than "I," be focused and dynamic, keep personal details to yourself—bosses don't chatter or gossip about their social lives.

I guess what you have to do is be the grown-up and speak to the other workers as children. You become aloof and slightly withdrawn, mature and responsible, dependable and conscientious.

When I say aloof I do not mean arrogant. I'm sure you will have encountered lots of managers who make this simple mistake. Arrogance has no place at work. Arrogance is conceit and fake importance. Aloofness is being slightly withdrawn, being detached, being superior by dint of experience, skill, and natural ability.

> "BE FOCUSED AND DYNAMIC, KEEP PERSONAL DETAILS TO YOURSELF— BOSSES DON'T CHATTER OR GOSSIP ABOUT THEIR SOCIAL LIVES."

RULE 63

Act One Step Ahead

So. We've got you dressing one step up and talking one step up, now you have to act one step up. I know, I know, it's all too much, too hard, too difficult. Who said this was going to be easy? Not me, pal, I told you right from the word go that this was going to be hard—harder in fact than just doing the job like normal people. Being a Rules Player takes more effort, requires more attention to detail and is generally more like hard work than hard work. But the results are fantastic. In fact being a Rules Player automatically qualifies you for promotion—if you can be a Rules Player you deserve to be promoted. It's a sort of self-fulfilling prophecy. Carrying out the Rules requires strength of character, will power, determination, honesty, courage, experience, great talent, dedication, drive, nerve, and charisma—if you've got all these you'll be promoted anyway.

So, act one step up. Look at the way your boss enters the office. Notice anything? Watch the way they answer the phone, talk to staff, entertain customers, hold their pen, hang up their coat, open their office door, sit down, stand up—anything they do. I bet you'll notice that they move differently from, say the office junior or the maintenance team or the sales force or the marketing folk or the PR people.

> ## "CARRYING OUT THE RULES REQUIRES STRENGTH OF CHARACTER, WILL POWER, DETERMINATION, HONESTY, COURAGE, EXPERIENCE, GREAT TALENT, DEDICATION, DRIVE, NERVE, AND CHARISMA."

Acting one step up requires you to:

- Be more certain of yourself
- Be more mature
- Be more confident

You have to be languid and suave and sophisticated—no, no, not swaggering or aggressive. A simple exercise—do you have your own office? Do people knock on your door? What do you say? A mild "Come in, please"? or a one step up "Come." The higher you go the less time you have to waste. You get slicker and quicker, sleeker and fitter. You don't have time to waffle or use long expressions—a simple "Come" is more expedient. You too have to be expedient. That's the secret. Next.

Think One Step Ahead

We talked about being expedient. Thinking one step up is about thinking expediently. You don't have time to waste thinking:

- How will this affect my coffee breaks?
- Will this mean I can still have my vacation?
- Will I have to work harder? Longer?
- Will I score any kudos from this?

No, instead you will think:

- Is this better for the department?
- Will the company do well out of this?
- Can we bosses sell this to the work force?
- Are our customers going to be happy with this?

Get the message? See the point? You will start to think like a boss and less like a worker. You will see things from the company's point of view and not how it affects your own personal petty little desk footprint:

- See the big picture
- See the entire picture
- Picture the picture

- Direct the picture
- Produce the picture
- Stop being an extra

I guess these rules teach you how to be an individual, how to think for yourself, how to stand on your own two feet. But if you could do all that you wouldn't need these rules. And if you can't, can these rules teach you? Yes, of course they can. Read on.

> "YOU WILL START TO THINK LIKE A BOSS AND LESS LIKE A WORKER."

Address Corporate Issues and Problems

We talked about looking at things from the company's point of view and not from your own. You have to take this further and talk only about corporate issues and problems even when you are talking to yourself or close colleagues. You have to convince them you are already a boss—*see Rule 69*.

I remember doing my first book and naturally being terribly concerned with the look of it—did the cover look right, feel right, smell right? The marketing manager, obviously getting fed up with the interminable dreary phone calls from me to check up on every little detail, finally said, "Cans of beans, dear boy, cans of beans." I didn't know what he meant and he had to explain it all in words of one syllable. Each book is a product—a can of beans—it sits on a shelf and gets bought or not bought depending on factors over which I, the mere little cog writer, have no control such as the position of the book on the shelves, the competition stationed nearby, the weather, any discounts the bookstore happens to be offering, and on and on and on. All of these things, including fascinating things, such as how the color of the cover can affect sales. It was my job to supply the text and then to start thinking about

> ## "IF THE COMPANY SUGGESTS A NEW PROCEDURE, IMMEDIATELY THINK HOW IT AFFECTS YOUR CUSTOMERS AND NOT YOU."

the corporate issues such as how many cans of beans get sold in any accounting period, what my percentage share of any can of beans is, what the next can of beans will be, and can we sell them spaghetti next time?

When problems crop up it is easy to see things from your own point of view—how it directly affects you. Once you make the leap to corporate speak it gets easier to stop doing this and to start seeing problems from the company's point of view. This doesn't mean you have to become a company person hook, line, and sinker. In fact you are allowed to be honest and express your opinion. If it stinks it stinks—and you should say so. But say so from the company's point of view and not your own.

If the company suggests a new procedure, immediately think how it affects your customers and not you.

Talk of "We" Rather Than "I"

I once worked for a boss who asked who we worked for. We said:

- Ourselves
- Our families
- Our bank managers
- Our self esteem
- Our boss
- The management
- The company board of directors
- The customers
- The IRS
- The government

He said a polite "No" to all of these. He explained we worked for the shareholders. That's it. That's who you work for. Now go and buy some of your company's shares. Now you work for yourself. Now you can start to say "we" and "us" instead of "me" and "I" and that sort of thing.

You are now a shareholder so when you have to talk about company procedure you can think how it will affect us, the shareholders—and not them, the staff (of whom you used to be one, not so very long ago).

If you go to meetings it is so much more grown up (and cool) to talk of "we" instead of "I."

"If we are going to implement this new procedure, we need to appraise the junior staff's reaction first," instead of "I think this sucks."

"We ought to prioritize some time for talking about the exhibition"—instead of "I'm panicking, this darn exhibition is only two weeks away and I've done nothing."

> ## "IF YOU GO TO MEETINGS IT IS SO MUCH MORE GROWN UP (AND COOL) TO TALK OF 'WE' INSTEAD OF 'I.'"

RULE 67

Walk the Walk

Now you've got to put the whole package together—you've got to walk the walk. You've got to become whoever and whatever it is you aspire to be. This isn't mimicry but training. If you can't walk the walk, you can't do the job.

Remember though what we said right from the outset—you have to be able to come up with the goods, you must be able to do the job—and do it well. That is the bottom line. If you can't do the job leave the stage.

These rules are not for the bullshitters or the posers. They are for the really industrious, the talented, the hardworking, the naturally gifted, those who are prepared to put in some effort and burn some oil.

Study the job that you aspire to. Who is doing it now? Learn to think of them as the person who is doing *your* job. How are they handling it? Learn to appraise those who are senior to you in the way that they appraise you. Don't moan or whine about how your boss does the job—observe instead their mistakes and learn and profit from them. Watch where they go wrong and swear never to make the same mistakes. Watch what they do superbly well and start practicing their smart moves now.

If you are going to walk your walk you have to have the right mannerisms, the right dress code, the right way of speaking,

> ## "YOU'VE GOT TO BECOME WHOEVER AND WHATEVER IT IS YOU ASPIRE TO BE."

the right way of acting, the right responses and the right attitude. You only get these if you are prepared to put in some time carrying out a four-point plan:

- Watching
- Learning
- Practicing
- Incorporating

If you are prepared to do these four things you will fly. Of course, you also have to do these without anyone knowing what you are doing—as well as doing your normal everyday job as well. Tough order? Of course. Who said it was going to be easy?

RULE 68

Spend More Time with Senior Staff

No matter what level you are in the company you can spend time with senior members of staff and they won't even realize if you handle it right. Draw attention to yourself and you will be spotted as an interloper, a spy, an intruder, a gatecrasher. Remember as a small child you could attend grown-up parties if you stayed quiet. They forgot you were there. Once spotted you got carried off to bed—where you belonged. It's the same as a junior. You can hang around and learn, but don't blow it or you'll be sent back to bed metaphorically.

When I was an office junior I noticed that senior members of staff tended to hang back after meetings sort of chewing the fat among themselves. The juniors scuttled off leaving these bigwigs to chat. I found that if I hung around also, sort of tidying up the table, emptying ashtrays (those were the days), and keeping quiet, then I got to overhear a lot and was even consulted on the odd occasion—"Ah, Richard, you're part of the new invoicing procedures, what do you think of them?" This was my chance to shine. I blew it of course and stammered and blushed and was tongue-tied and useless. Next time I got it better and eventually got it right.

There came a time when I was asked something and I was coherent, confident, and mature. Strange that I was also whisked up the promotion ladder quite rapidly very soon after. This was when I was working for a very old-fashioned British company and their promotion route was very fixed, you had to follow a very set procedure. I was allowed to bypass this system and I put it all down to hanging around the top guns.

Sometimes you will notice a boss sitting on their own at a lunch or social occasion. Most "workers" are too nervous to go up to them and chat or so entrenched in their social circle that they can't talk to them. Forget that. Go up and make small talk. You'll be amazed how often bosses are grateful for a "worker" talking to them because they too are human and feel isolated, lonely, ignored, forgotten. They are glad of a chat, just so long as you don't take advantage and ask about a raise or time off or your vacation time. But it is OK to ask about their experiences—"So how did you get into marketing, Ms Johnson?"

You may well find you pick up useful hints and tips as well as getting ready for the next rule—Getting people to assume you have already made the step.

Get People to Assume You Have Already Made the Step

Act like a general manager and people will accept you as one. Act like an office junior and that's what people will think you are. So how are we going to get people to make this assumption?

- Be confident and assertive and sound mature: "Yes, we can do that—I'll make sure we get on to that immediately."

- If you come to work wearing tennis shoes and a sweatshirt you won't command the same respect as you would if you wore a smart business suit and looked the part.

- If you talk of "I" and refer every problem back to how it affects you—"I can't work through my lunch break, I'm entitled to my hour off"—instead of "We" and seeing things from the company's point of view, what's best for the whole organization—"We need to pull together here, I'm happy to work through lunch to help us get this problem solved."

- If you talk about what you watched on TV last night and where you are going on vacation and what you are going to do at the weekend, you come across as more lightweight—and thus junior—than if you talked about company issues, what your department's plans are for the future, how the rise in interest rates is going to affect business over the next few months and what you are going to do about exchange rates and the dollar.

Basically what you have to do is get people to recognize you as a heavyweight and not a lightweight. Be serious, mature, grown up and adult. This doesn't mean you have to be a geek, a nerd, a suck-up, a goody-goody, or a bore. You can still take a joke, enjoy a laugh, smile, be lighthearted and jovial, be fun and full of life. You need to project a mature but fun image. You need to make people aware that you:

- Know the job
- Are experienced
- Are serious
- Are reliable and responsible
- Are trustworthy
- Are the job you want to be

So, take to sauntering around the place looking suave and cool and being very stylish and grown up, make the appropriate noises and make sure that when you get offered the job you are after that you can already do it.

Prepare for the Step After Next

Sorry but you can't coast. You are a Rules Player now and you must stick at it—no days off, no rests, no breaks, no putting your feet up drinking coffee and staring into space. Back to the grindstone. So, you've got your eye on the next step, the next job. Fine, good. But what about after that? What's your next step? What's your next target?

Even before you've got your next promotion you should already be practicing for the next step. Because if you aren't getting ready now, when will you be? There is always an opportunity to miss a step out, to skip over a promotion if you play this game well. I'm not suggesting this should always be your aim, but be prepared just in case it happens.

Of course you have your long- and short-term plans—*Part 3*— so you will have plotted your career path and know the steps you have to take on your great journey. Even now you will be getting people to assume you have already made the next step, acting the part of the next step, walking your walk, and talking as if you were already the boss, but it doesn't hurt to start practicing for the step after that.

Letting people see that you are officer material is no bad thing. Once people get in the habit of assuming you are a high flier you become one. If you dress down, talk trivia, don't pull your weight and act like you are a bore or a drone you will get accepted as that—and stay right where you are.

Look around the office. Can you spot the bores and the drones? The worker ants? The plodders and the sloggers? Now look again and spot the high fliers, the heavyweights, the go-getters, the live wires. Can you see the difference? Can you see what you have to do? Can you see how acting the part makes you that part? Can you? Can you?

Whatever step you are preparing for, make sure that everything you do is genuine, real, and worthwhile. I once worked with a young man who was a high flier. He was preparing for his next step. He took to coming to work carrying a briefcase when none of his colleagues did—none of us needed one. Trouble is Ray's briefcase fell open one day and revealed to the entire world that all it contained was his sandwiches, a newspaper, and a set of keys. It was humiliating for him, embarrassing for us, and sad for everyone. Make sure your briefcase is full of real stuff just in case this—or anything like it—happens to you.

PART 8

CULTIVATE DIPLOMACY

Smooth Rules Players move rapidly up the corporate ladder because they are diplomats. They don't start fights, they stop them. They don't sit on fences, they mend them. They spread calm around them and others turn to them for advice and inspiration. You too will be a diplomat. You will be known for your objective appraisal of any situation, your impartial attitude and your even-handed dealings.

RULE 71

Ask Questions in Times of Conflict

So you are at a meeting and things are getting hot under the collar. The chairman isn't handling things particularly well and Steve and Rachael are going for each other's throats yet again. What are you going to do? Ask questions. It is easy to defuse dangerous situations by getting the protagonists to look at some detail. You don't have to break up the fight—that's not your job. But you can be the diplomat, this gets you noticed and earns respect from your colleagues.

Turn to Steve and ask him, "Steve, why are you so convinced that your department is going to find these new invoices unworkable?" If Rachael carries on the fight just say to her, "Hang on Rach, I really want to hear what Steve has to say." You've made it clear that you aren't taking sides but you are diffusing the situation. Hear Steve out and then turn to Rachael. "You are convinced that Steve is wrong. Tell me why."

What you have effectively done is taken over the chair's role, become the head honcho, assumed control. This is both diplomatic and clever.

Asking questions invariably takes the heat out of potentially explosive situations. You turn to one of the combatants and ask them a simple question. Don't get bogged down in psycho-babble of the "Why do you feel like that?" "Can you share your anger with us?" Instead ask them to focus on an aspect that needs explaining. They will have to break eye contact with their opponent to think about answering you. Thus the heat dissipates and you have proved yourself as a diplomat.

Avoid doing this if either protagonist looks like the blood has drained from their face—white face means they will hit someone, red face merely blowing hot and hard.

Avoid doing this if the chairman is handling the situation effectively—obviously they aren't if the fight has started, but they may be making an effort and will resent your intrusion.

Avoid doing this if you are involved in the argument in any way personally.

Asking questions usually gets people to switch their attention from the main argument to a detail. They have to be pretty angry not to be polite enough to at least attempt to answer your question.

Don't Take Sides

If you take sides, then you are part of the argument, the fight, the dispute, the disagreement. You have to remain totally objective and firmly in the middle. Stay on the fence whatever you do, because if you don't, then one side will blame you as well as the person they were arguing with originally. Whatever the case up for discussion *you* need to:

- Take a long-term view
- See it from the company's point of view
- Remain impartial
- Remain calm
- Be the diplomat
- Not take sides
- Stay independent

The more detached you appear to be, the more senior you will come across. If you jump in with your boots on and take sides, you run the risk of making an enemy as well as being seen as hot-headed.

The difficulty is when a friend is embroiled in a row with another less-close colleague. Your friend will invariably turn to you and try to drag you in, "Oh, for God's sake, tell her I'm right will you Rich?"

You can't afford to be dragged in. You will have to hold your hands up defensively and say, "Don't involve me. If you two can't sort this out sensibly and without arguing I will send you both to your room." Here you have:

- Made a joke of it thus lessening the tension
- Indicated that you are senior to both of them
- Remained uninvolved
- Not taken sides

> "STAY ON THE FENCE WHATEVER YOU DO, BECAUSE IF YOU DON'T, THEN ONE SIDE WILL BLAME YOU AS WELL AS THE PERSON THEY WERE ARGUING WITH ORIGINALLY."

Know When to Keep Your Opinions to Yourself

It's very easy to have opinions. We all have them. Trouble is knowing when to keep them to yourself and when to express them. The reason most people don't know when to shut up is that they think their opinion:

- Counts for something
- Has an audience
- Is important
- Will make a difference
- Will make them seem clever/intelligent/effective
- Will win them approval/love/attention

All of these, of course, are the wrong reasons for expressing an opinion. The real reason for expressing an opinion is because you have been asked to. If you are asked, then say what you think. If you ain't been asked, then shut up.

Your opinion should almost have to be dragged from you. What you have to say is important and you don't squander

> ## "THE REAL REASON FOR EXPRESSING AN OPINION IS BECAUSE YOU HAVE BEEN ASKED TO."

your opinions willy nilly. You don't run off at the mouth. You don't sit there spouting opinions. You do:

- Have an opinion ready for when you are asked
- Learn to express that opinion clearly and precisely and accurately
- Always make it sound as if your opinion isn't just an opinion but the actual solution that will be implemented

The way to make your opinion seem less like an opinion and more like an accepted fact is to express it as a fact. Don't say, "I think we should," instead say, "We should." Don't say, "In my opinion the ZX300 is a good machine." Instead say "The ZX300 is a good machine."

So avoid:

- I think
- I feel
- In my opinion

Be Conciliatory

Feathers have been ruffled. You weren't involved. It was nothing to do with you. Doesn't matter. Make sure it is you who soothes those feathers.

- Make everyone a cup of coffee.
- Stroke a few egos.
- Clear the air.
- Open a window.
- Get them to shake hands (or kiss and make up).

If feathers have been ruffled by a boss telling off a junior, make sure it is the junior you comfort, cheer up, brighten up, perk up, whatever. The boss should be handled differently. The best way is the silent but disapproving action of conciliation— make them a cup of coffee but say nothing. You are indicating that you disapprove—and thus are really senior to them because you wouldn't make such a mistake—that you aren't scared of them or their anger or whatever. But maintain the silence.

If you do this well they will be obliged to ask you what you thought of the way they blew up or shouted or disciplined someone. Just say, "It isn't really for me to say, is it?" Invariably they will say, "I would value your opinion," or "No, I'd like to know," or "It's OK, say what you think." It doesn't matter what they say, you've got them.

Now you can be conciliatory, now you can be the diplomat, now you have turned the tables. Just say, 'You handled it fine. Trish was out of order and she needed telling." Don't, whatever you do, actually criticize the way they handled things. Let them know you disapprove but never, ever admit that in real life.

Always remember that your job isn't to make waves but to ride them. Surf your way to the top by being conciliatory. By doing this you will win friends, bring together opposing sides and gain respect.

Being conciliatory is a bit like breaking up fights between kids. You don't want to know who started it—no, you really don't— or what it is about. You don't want the details of who pinched who, or who bit who. All you want is peace restored and for them to shake hands and start over again being friends. That, at work, is all you want too. Use the same techniques you would use on small children.

Never Lose Your Temper

I don't care how annoying Pete in marketing can be, or how riled you get when Sandra from R & D plays jokes or how high your blood pressure rises when the accounting department messes up yet again—you will not ever, under any circumstances lose your temper. That's it. There are no exceptions. No small breaches. No thin end of any wedges. You will not lose your temper.

Not unless, of course, it is entirely staged, for effect. Then you are allowed to do it. But you have to be very careful that you have chosen the right moment, the right occasion, and the right person for an audience.

But if it ain't staged then you don't do it. And I don't care how angry they make you or how annoying they can be or how justified you think you are. Loss of temper means loss of control. And the one thing a Rules Player has is control.

So how do you sit on your hands? How do you learn how to be calm and well behaved? Easy. Raise your eyes to the heavens. No, seriously. You only lose your temper if you are involved, if you care, if you are part of the problem. If you shift your focus to higher issues—the old good of the company again—it becomes easier to see whatever it is that is annoying you in a new light.

Another method is to simply leave the office or meeting or whatever. Just say, "I find this situation intolerable." And then leave. It creates quite a shock and usually does the trick.

Or try counting to ten while you sit on your hands.

Not losing your temper doesn't mean not expressing emotion. You are entitled to say, "I find it extremely annoying when you eat all the chocolate cookies/lose the invoices/upset another major customer/park in the manager's parking space/steal the petty cash"—whatever it is that drives you nuts.

It is OK to refuse to give in to emotional blackmail or bullying or over-assertive behavior or whining. It is not OK to bottle up stuff. Say when you feel aggrieved, immediately, so that you defuse the situation at once. Don't let things build up a head of steam or you may well blow. Let it out bit by bit and it shouldn't ever come to a head.

Never Get Personal

It is their behavior that is wrong or annoying or detrimental to the department. It is never them. And it is never annoying to you, only to the good of the department. The key way to remember this is a dreadful New Age thing that crept in from American parenting stuff. They say, "She isn't a naughty girl; she's a good girl who has done a naughty thing." Yuk. Or how about, "He is a good boy who has done a bad thing?"

This sets the scene though. It isn't the person, it is their behavior. You never ever get personal.

You can criticize:

- The way they do their job
- Their time keeping, their attitude
- Their motivation
- Their communication skills
- Their long-term goals
- Their focus
- Their knowledge of office procedures
- Their appreciation of company policy
- Their interpersonal skills
- Their productivity output

But you can't *ever* say they are a lazy, ignorant, good for nothing, lying, thieving bitching bastard. Oh no. Not ever. They may need retraining, relocating, re-educating, redirecting, remotivating but never being told exactly what you really, really think of them. Getting personal will get you fired at worst and lose you respect and friends at best.

The same goes for your boss. You may know they are useless, incompetent, corrupt, and stupid. But can you say so? No. Not even to colleagues. Remember what we said about sticking up for junior members of staff or the underdog or anyone that everyone else is attacking? Well, your boss is the same. You always stick up for them—no matter what. You do not get personal about them, with them or around them.

> "GETTING PERSONAL WILL GET YOU FIRED AT WORST AND LOSE YOU RESPECT AND FRIENDS AT BEST."

Know How to Handle Other People's Anger

There will be times when you really annoy other people. In fact, being a Rules Player may irk them even if they haven't a clue what it is you are doing. No one likes a smartass and you might be seen as one if you cut loose from the herd and start looking good and looking cool. They may confront you. They may like to take a swing at you. How do you defuse their anger?

First you have to understand that there is two types of anger:

- Justified anger
- Tactical anger

Justified anger is exactly that—justified. You just ran over their foot in your car because you weren't looking. They are quite justifiably angry. What do you do? You get out of the car and apologize. Say, and mean, that you are sorry. Don't deny it was your fault. Don't tell them it is nothing and they are making a bit of a fuss and you once had your entire leg ripped off and never even noticed. Don't try and explain why you weren't looking where you were going. Don't try to brush off the whole thing—"I'd have thought you'd have been pleased to have had your foot run over by a top of the range Mercedes." And for God's sake don't laugh.

Justifiable anger needs a result. If you have done something wrong listen to them—they are angry. You have made them so. Listen to what you have done wrong. And then apologize and find some way to put things right. Show the person that you sympathize—you may not be able to give them what they want but you can still let them know that you appreciate their feelings. Don't brush their feelings aside—they are justified.

Tactical anger is, however, another thing entirely. Tactical anger is used to make you do things you don't want to. People lose their temper to intimidate you. The worst thing you can do is let them get away with it. If you do, they'll keep doing it, to you and to others. You must stop them at once. The way to do this is simply to say, "I don't like being shouted at/threatened/ intimidated/bullied/whatever, and I shall leave if you don't stop/calm down/put your fists down/let go of my throat," whatever.

If they continue then just leave. That's it. Say nothing, just walk out of the room. Do this often enough and they get the message.

Stand Your Ground

No one is allowed to bully you, threaten you, shout at you, hit you, intimidate you, frighten you, tease you, victimize you, or torment you in any way. You are an employee. If you aren't doing your job properly, you should be taken to one side and have your mistakes pointed out calmly and rationally. Anything else is abuse.

You are allowed to refuse abuse. You are allowed, calmly and rationally, to tell them to stop at once or you are entitled to use the full weight of the law to get them to stop. You have to know when to stand your ground.

Obviously if they are mildly teasing—the same as everyone else gets—then you can't walk out and claim unfair dismissal. If your boss snaps at you occasionally—the same as they do to all employees—you can't demand the courts string them up, even if they are out of order. If a colleague says they'll give you a slap if you steal their hole puncher again you can't really expect the Supreme Court to take up your case. We are talking real abuse here, not the sort of rough and tumble you'd expect in the hurly burly of a busy working life.

Standing your ground is about having standards, drawing a line in the sand and saying, "I will put up with this, but not this', or "I will allow them to do this to me, but not this."

Standing your ground is about being assertive. Being assertive is about confidently stating your bottom line:

- I won't be spoken to like that.
- I am feeling threatened and bullied and shall leave the room.
- I don't appreciate being locked in dark closets and I shall have to report this incident to my union representative/ boss/the police/the Health and Safety committee/ my mother.

If bullied, stick to the stuck record—"I don't appreciate being treated like this. I don't appreciate being treated like this. I don't appreciate being treated like this." Don't lose your temper, or they may feel they have "won." Walk away.

Be Objective About the Situation

If you are feeling attacked, abused, tormented at work you have various choices:

- Walk
- Report it
- Flair up and be angry
- Say nothing
- Handle it assertively

How you choose to handle difficult situations is entirely up to you. However, before you react, think of the long-term plan. How will a claim for unfair dismissal or constructive dismissal look on your resumé over a career history? I'm not saying you should put up with abuse of any sort just to advance your career. No, I am not saying that at all. I am saying be objective about the situation.

I was once ridiculed by a particular boss—and badly ridiculed. This man had got it into his head that I was his pet football to be kicked around as and when he felt like it—and that was, curiously, often after boozy lunches. I was quite junior and had few choices—walk away from the job or go over his head and report him. But his boss was also his best friend. If I reported him I would have been out on my ear pretty quick. I needed the job and didn't want to walk away. I had to be quite devious, but I basically got him to treat me badly—ridiculing, abusive language, that sort of thing—when one of our major customers was listening.

My boss didn't know this and the customer was furious. He let my boss have it in no uncertain terms. Said he ought to be ashamed of himself treating a junior like that. Put him in his place and then told me to tell him if this ever happened again—and that if it did he would take his business elsewhere. His business was about 70 percent of our entire turnover.

My boss had to apologize to me in front of the customer. And I wasn't treated badly again. I felt I was objective. I then waited, and sure enough he screwed up again with someone else and was eventually fired. I waved goodbye to him with a cheery grin and a wink.

Put Things in Perspective

When all is said and done, it is only a job. It ain't your health, your love life, your family, your children, your life or your soul. If, by the way, it is any of these things then you really have gone badly wrong along the way.

Your job is just a job. Yes, I know you need the money etc., etc. But it is just a job and there are others.

Having a bad day at work shouldn't cause you to:

- Lose sleep
- Lose your appetite
- Lose your sex drive
- Smoke more
- Drink more
- Take drugs
- Be more irritable
- Get depressed
- Get stressed

But you'd be surprised how often these things are done by people because they have had a bad day. Yes, they may have had a whole series of bad days. But taken one by one, it is just a bad day. You have to learn to switch off, relax, not take it so seriously, enjoy it more, put things into perspective.

Get a hobby, get a life. You must work to live, not live to work. Don't take stuff home with you—learn to be assertive and say no. Put your family first. Spend time with your children—they will grow up so fast you will miss their precious childhood if you work your way through it—believe me I have seen my children grow up and it is so swift it is terrifying. It may seem slow and stressful at the time, but it zips past and then is irrecoverably gone—and you missed it because you were doing paperwork of an evening or attending another boring conference at the weekend.

It is just a job.

> "YOU HAVE TO LEARN TO SWITCH OFF, RELAX, NOT TAKE IT SO SERIOUSLY, ENJOY IT MORE, PUT THINGS INTO PERSPECTIVE."

KNOW THE SYSTEM— AND MILK IT

If you are going to move on up, you had better know the ropes. Part 9 teaches you how to understand the system—and how to milk it for all you're worth. This rule will have you outmanaging the management because you'll know the system better than they do.

Know All the Unspoken Rules of Office Life

There are a whole lot of unwritten rules in any work place. These might be as simple as who is "allowed" to use which elevator/lunchroom/bathroom/corridor/outside smoking area, or as complex as who holds the keys to the petty cash/photocopier/stationery cupboard/vacation schedules. I have often known the strangest people doing duties which no one has ever given them. I once worked in an office where a Swiss translator was in charge of the vacation schedules. Why, for heaven's sake?

You had to get your vacation approved by her, logged by her, and permitted by her. But why her? Whenever I asked I was told it was historical that the translators did the vacations. It was bizarre, stupid, really off the wall. My supervisor should have done them, but I guess he was quite pleased that the translators had taken this "burden" off his shoulders. Weird.

If you have been in your job for a while you should have learned all these rules by now. If new, then these things are waiting to be found out. OK, so you know these rules, what use are they to you? Easy. It's a bit like the unions used to be—working to an obscure rule book that the management

> **"IF YOU HAVE BEEN IN YOUR JOB FOR A WHILE YOU SHOULD HAVE LEARNED ALL THESE RULES BY NOW. IF NEW, THEN THESE THINGS ARE WAITING TO BE FOUND OUT."**

never really understood or knew. You will be able to out-maneuver anyone by knowing these unwritten rules.

I went to work in an office where the most junior had to take the most senior boss his coffee in the mornings and the unwritten rule was that this junior would wait while he drank the coffee. The junior didn't "have" to, it was just expected of him. I was that junior. For about five minutes every day I had the ultimate boss's undivided attention. I had the ear of the highest. I had access to God. I milked it, as you might have guessed.

I got my department head moved to another department. He was unpopular and I merely mentioned to the big boss that the department head had certain skills that he hadn't revealed, but which would come in very useful in the new department. He was moved.

RULE 82

Know What to Call Everyone

Yes, you should know what to call everyone, but that doesn't mean you are going to call them it. I dare say Mr Cutler has long since forgotten me. I was his assistant many years ago. When he changed company he phoned me and asked me to join the new firm with him—more money etc.—so I said yes.

On my first day working with him at the new company he said to me, "Call me Mr Cutler." No way, Peter. I had called him Peter at the old place and was going to carry on calling him that. But not quite yet. There were several assistants and they needed to get to know this new boss, this Mr Cutler. That's what they called him, because that's what he wanted. I waited until the moment was right and we were all gathered together. Then I addressed him as Peter.

He couldn't cut me down to size in front of my peers and they thought, quite rightly, that I had secret access to him that they didn't. For me the Mr Cutler nonsense was never mentioned again and I was the "senior" assistant because I called him Peter. What's in a name? A whole lot.

You need to know that Mrs Robertson in accounting is always addressed as Mrs Robertson and never as Mary, although you know that is her name and you are senior to her. Why not call her Mary? Because she doesn't like it and she handles the wage checks. They have been known to go astray, be very late, be made out for much less than the anticipated amount—and all to people who inadvertently called her Mary.

In one job, I worked with an administrative manager who was known, for curious reasons, as Buckethead. It's a long story and you really don't want to know (no, believe me you really don't). He was addressed to his face as Buckethead by all the senior staff—including me as Finance Manager. He was Buckethead to the board. He was Buckethead to most of the secretarial staff. But anyone else and he was Mr Taylor, never Buckethead. I have seen him savage a young junior who made the mistake and called him Buckethead. Now why this strange division between who could and who could not call him it? I have no idea but I did have a very strange relationship with him. Technically he was my senior, albeit it only slightly. But I was power hungry in those days and I wanted to control everything. I never ever called him Buckethead. I didn't like him. To me he was always Mr Taylor. Why? Because it separated us and made me different from the other senior managers. I stood alone and Buckethead could never get close to me, never be a "friend." I played the aloof game and was eventually offered the General Managership of the company which would have made him my junior. Success? Yes, but it felt a hollow victory—I wasn't playing the Rules as effectively then as now—and I left for new challenges, new horizons.

Know When to Stay Late and When to Go Early

There is an unwritten rule that if you want to advance you have to stay late because everyone else stays late. Clones stay late. Drones stay late. Worker ants stay late. Rules Players go home when they want to—and that is invariably earlier than anyone else.

It's the same with arriving in the office in the morning. Who says you have to arrive early? No one. It is one of those unwritten rules we need to know, so we can adapt it to our own ends.

The object of the exercise is to be *thought* to be working as hard as everyone else. The game is to get away with being thought of as a conformist, a drone, when in fact you don't have to because you are so much better than that. You get your work done in record time so you don't have to stay late.

If you ever watch motivational speakers, they always put their hand up when they ask you—and the rest of the audience—a question. This sets the lead and you automatically put your hand up because there is already one hand up in the room. Silly isn't it? But it only takes one of you to leave at a reasonable time for everyone else to follow suit. Staying because you think everyone else is staying is called "presenteeism" and is a curse of modern office life. We all think that everyone else is watching us, as we are watching them, to see who will be the first to break, to leave, to incur the boss's wrath.

It is however a myth. The first to leave isn't going to be missing anything. They will be liberating the rest of us. Leave now and set us free, please.

The fear of missing something is very real. But if we are leading exciting and interesting lives, we know that we are the center of the universe and that the others who stay behind are the ones who are in reality missing out, missing something, missing in action.

People think that leaving early—or at the right time actually, the time we are contracted to leave—will draw undue attention to us, make us seem to be shirkers or slackers. But if we leave confidently and honestly this doesn't happen. We only get viewed badly for leaving before others if we slink out, leave by the back door, creep away into the night with our tail between our legs. So wave boldly and tell them, "Last one to leave turns out the lights." Whether it is fair to point out that if they were any good at their jobs they too, like you, would have finished their work on time is debatable. You are allowed to think it though.

RULE 84

Know the Theft or Perks Rule

So what can you take home? Pens? Paperclips? Staplers? When is it a perk and when is it theft? You should know this, as it can come in useful if you want to have a hold over someone—the someone who thinks nothing of taking home everything that ain't actually screwed down. Watch what they take and make a mental note of it. This might come in useful. You, of course, will take nothing.

I have known an entire department cleared out because a new manager suddenly got it into his head that they were all committing grand larceny because they took home copies of all the software used by the computers. At home they all had the latest Windows, Word, and Outlook Express but a fat lot of good it did them when they had to sign on.

Was it theft? It doesn't matter. It got them fired. If one of them had been known not to do this, they would have survived. If one of them had known the new manager's views on perks they might have survived.

Before you start filling your pockets, make sure it is worth it. Are those pens really that attractive? Will you be able to sell enough cheap file folders to feed your family for however long it takes you to find a new job?

Earlier we looked at the unwritten rules of office life. It might well be such a rule that you do take home perks. And if you choose not to, make sure you don't get labeled as a teacher's pet or goody goody or anything else that could get you ostracized. Be part of the herd even if you steal nothing. Let your boss know you don't, but make the staff think you are the same as them.

And watch out for the free phone calls and the Internet connection. These might not qualify as take-home perks but it is still theft to make free phone calls when you aren't allowed to. There is a good chance they get monitored, so don't do it.

Padding expenses can be part of the office culture. If you don't do it, it can blow the whistle on the others who do. So what do you do? You have to be honest and above board but you can't rat on your colleagues. Ask the audience? Phone a friend? Doing it might seem the lesser of two evils, but you are a Rules Player now and can't condone such activity. Better to say in advance to your colleagues that they can do what they like or want but you won't be a party to such irregularities. Warn them beforehand and then if they still insist on doing it, you haven't spilled the beans.

Identify the People Who Count

I once made a bad mistake—well, I've probably made lots, but this one is relevant and sticks in my mind. I worked for a company and we had a maintenance man. At the end of each day, we wrote in the maintenance book anything that needed doing, such as changing light bulbs, clearing blocked toilets and Harry would do it. Mending broken chairs, that sort of thing. We had two offices and I used to get quite cross that Harry seemed to spend more time down at the other branch than at our place. Harry was never anywhere to be found.

My notes in the maintenance book grew terse and sharper, but it didn't seem to do any good. I would have told off Harry in person if ever I'd have been able to find him. He came in after we had gone home and did the maintenance work in the evenings. The other office was getting all their repairs done and we were getting nothing done. It was intolerable and I resolved one evening to wait for Harry.

Harry didn't show, so I went over to the other office. There was Harry having coffee with the big boss, my regional director. I steamed in—"What the devil do you think you're doing? I need you over at the other place doing maintenance, not sitting here drinking coffee!" Bad mistake. Several bad mistakes:

- You don't bawl someone out for drinking coffee when they were on an official "coffee break."

- You don't bawl someone out for drinking coffee when they have been invited to do so by the regional director.

- You don't bawl someone out in front of your regional director without first checking all the salient facts with them.

- You do things properly—go through the appropriate channels and don't hide in wait for an errant worker.

- You always *identify the people who count*—in this case, Harry.

Why did Harry count? Because he was my regional director's father-in-law. He had juice and power and influence that I could only dream of. He was working at the other office because he had been told to by his son-in-law. As I said, bad mistake.

I've worked for companies where it was the cashier, the managing director's driver, the accountant, and the cafeteria chef who had the juice. Invariably, it took some time to identify these people. They all held some trump card which either gave them access to a senior boss, or some hold over them such as being a relative. Find them, know them.

Be on the Right Side of the People Who Count

So how do you think I got on with Harry after my outburst? Our relationship was bad beforehand. Now it positively stank. Do you think I could get a light bulb changed? No way, not now, not ever. Identifying the people who count and being on the right side of them go hand in hand, obviously.

I once worked with an auditor who was a complete you-know-what. Everything had to be done by the book. Every i dotted and t crossed. This man would have made Attila the Hun look like a charity worker. But this was a man who counted. Not only was he the auditor, he seemed to have juice far beyond his role as an accountant. This was a man the senior management bowed to, listened to, sought advice from, dared not cross, were in fear of, and they generally treated him like royalty.

I never quite got to the bottom of why he wielded so much influence but I had to work with it. And once I had identified him I had to get on the right side of him. I hadn't been up to then. As finance manager my department came under his scrutiny constantly and closely.

I had upset him at every step along the way. We didn't see eye to eye. He was an accountant and I was a finance manager—there is quite a difference. My brief was to install security systems, improve cash flow, cut costs, and tighten all fiscal procedures. His was to audit every penny.

I took my kids to a garage sale one Saturday morning. It was autumn and I felt cold so I bought a college scarf at the sale. You know the sort, stripy, dark, traditional. On Monday I wore it into work. I bumped into the auditor in the corridor. "Ah," he said "I didn't know you went to Notre Dame. Well done." And he walked off.

I hadn't a clue what he was talking about until it dawned on me that the scarf was a Notre Dame scarf. This was the university the auditor had gone to (no, I hadn't gone there, or to any university) and from then on he accepted me as one of his own, a chum, an old college pal. I could do no wrong.

This was an accident. Since then I have engineered such incidents to get on the right side of the people who count, the ones who have influence who shouldn't. These are the ones who have juice incommensurate with their position or job.

There is a group of people you should watch out for—they often have unaccountable juice—which includes: drivers, auditors, PR people, Human Resource people, PAs, people who have been with the company for a very long time, outside consultants, free agents, cashiers, ex-employees, and of course maintenance people!

Be Aware of New Management Techniques

You cannot afford ever to stand still, to rest on your laurels, to sit back and take it easy. All the time you are doing any of these things there will be someone stealing a march on you.

You have to move with the times and that means keeping up with the latest management techniques, the newest buzz-words, whatever is executive flavor of the month. To stay on top you have to know what jargon is being talked. It's no good referring to it as personnel when everyone else is talking about human resources. You'll look a chump if you are still stuck in logistics when the board are now concentrating on client-focused core business or whatever.

I'm not suggesting you have to use these new techniques but you had better know them to stay ahead of the pack—you may be asked. You can always have fun playing buzzword bingo at meetings—award yourself a point for every new ridiculous buzzword you hear and when you have ten points leap to your feet and shout, "Bingo!" It keeps you awake.

And you'll certainly hear a lot of wonderfully useless expressions—for instance what exactly does Blue Sky mean? As in, "We shall have to Blue Sky this product." It might mean, "anything goes, be creative and set no boundaries." It might also mean, "We're a bunch of jargonists who want to sound cool and with it, but who actually sound rather silly."

If you use buzzwords try not to sound silly. You should, of course, know what they all mean.

You should also know what all the latest management disciplines are and how they might affect you. Try not to sound out of date when you talk of management techniques. For instance it was called logistics in my day, but now it is supply chain management—and by the time you are reading this it will be something else I expect.

You should know what the advantages and disadvantages of any of these buzzwords are just in case they crop up and you want to look good. There ought to be a sort of bluffer's guide to management speak, but I don't think there is, so you will have to incorporate it into your game plan and see the big picture because at the end of the day there will be a new ball park and the best practice of your core business will be a sort of knock-on effect that will play you out of the loop if you don't take your knowledge off-line and start thinking outside of the box which might just get you in with the movers and shakers without having to move your goal posts or go the extra mile while playing hardball and being a showstopper. So stretch the envelope and the bottom line is total quality.

RULE 88

Know the Undercurrents and Hidden Agendas

When your boss says he wants to improve customer relations and you should all go on a course to learn how to smile don't be fooled. It's nothing to do with smiling at customers. Your boss is coming up for appraisal time and needs to look good, needs to appear as if there is some drive, initiative, and motivation.

So you'll all troop off and do the course and try to take it all in and practice your smile. What for? Your boss couldn't give two monkeys whether you smile at the customers or not. All they want is to shine at their appraisal.

This sort of thing goes on a lot more at work than most people like to think. Once, I volunteered to attend college every Monday to do a course in payroll and double entry book-keeping. My boss thought I was keen, self-motivated, and very enthusiastic. Nonsense. I wanted to get out of the office every Monday because that was the day we had to do all the filing and I hated it. Going to college seemed a good excuse.

Question the motives of everyone and everything. This doesn't mean you have to become paranoid. No one is out to get you. All you need to do is watch out for the hidden agenda. It might not affect you in any way but it will be fun to spot what is really going on.

I once worked for a boss who always liked to be the last to leave. I thought him conscientious and industrious. It was only when he had been arrested for fraud that I realized that staying, after everyone else had gone, was his opportunity to cook the books. And there was little old me admiring his keen spirit.

Always ask:

- Why is this happening?
- Is there anything I am missing?
- Who benefits from this?
- How are they benefiting?
- What else could be going on?
- Can I benefit from this?
- How?

As I said don't get paranoid, get the facts.

Know the Favorites and Cultivate Them

Every boss has a favorite. I know they/we shouldn't, but it is human nature. It goes on because we/they are all human and even parents have favorites although they would never admit it.

There are two parts to this rule:

* If favoritism is going on—and it will be—make sure you are your boss's favorite.

* Make sure you know all the favorites in other departments.

If you have got a boss who is going to have favorites, you can buck the system or try being the favorite. If you do become a favorite, don't for heaven's sake flaunt it among your colleagues. Be self-effacing and deny it, be humble and don't acknowledge it, be modest and pretend it ain't going on.

To get to be a favorite has to depend on skill, presence, charisma, talent, expertise, experience, likeability, charm, personal affability. It must never depend on brown nosing, fawning, obsequiousness, toadying, sliming, or smarming up to the boss. You have to earn being a favorite, not worm your way in. If you do, you will be hated by your colleagues. If you genuinely deserve it because you are dependable or reliable or efficient or honest, then your colleagues will just about put up with it.

Spotting the favorites in other departments should be fairly easy. They will be treated pretty much as you are. They will:

- Get the first pick on the vacation schedule
- Be trusted, a confidante
- Be invited to meetings
- Get the prestigious jobs and the perks
- Be chatted to by the boss rather than being barked at

Once spotted, make a friend of them. This way you will know what is going on, be in with the in-crowd, have the ear of the boss of other departments and have joined an elite. If, on the other hand, you really disapprove of favoritism do none of this.

RULE 90

Know the Mission Statement—and Understand it

In the good old days, a company's mission statement was probably "Make as much money as possible and keep the shareholders off our back." Not any more it ain't. A mission statement is now much more complex. If you want to make a success of your employment, you have to know and understand the mission statement—and then milk it for all you are worth. Quoting the mission statement earns you brownie points if you make sure it looks as if you are really on the side of the company. If your boss doesn't support the mission statement, or considers such things as rubbish and not worth bothering with, then keep quiet about mission statements.

To understand the mission statement is usually quite easy— Walt Disney's "To make people happy," Wal-Mart's "To give ordinary folk the chance to buy the same thing as rich people"—but to really understand it, you have to read all the small print. For instance Disney's is quite simple but there is a whole lot more because they also have a "value statement" which covers:

- No cynicism
- Creativity, dreams, and imagination
- Nurturing and promulgation of "wholesome American values"
- Fanatical attention to consistency and detail
- Preservation and control of the Disney "magic"

If you can't find something here—assuming you work for Disney—to milk, you aren't worthy of calling yourself a Rules Player. Imagine what fun you could have with some of these. Imagine what power you would wield at meetings just quoting some of this. Someone suggests an idea you don't like, you could just say it isn't wholesomely American. Brilliant. It's like being part of the Spanish Inquisition—our chief weapons are ... Among our many weapons are such diverse ....

Some historical mission statements were very grand and could have safely been milked for all they were worth:

- Ford (early 1900s)   Ford will democratize the automobile.
- Sony (early 1950s)—To become the company most known for changing the worldwide poor-quality image of Japanese products.
- Boeing (1950)—To become the dominant player in commercial aircraft and bring the world into the jet age.
- Wal-Mart (1990)—To become a $125 billion company by the year 2000.

PART 10

HANDLE THE OPPOSITION

If there's a promotion going and five possible candidates how do you identify them? And then how do you make yourself the obvious choice? Part 10 teaches you how to identify the competition—your competition. And then it teaches you how to make yourself the favorite without being ruthless or underhand. In fact if you practice this rule really well, you will get them to recommend you, and want you to be promoted ahead of them.

RULE 91

Identify the Opposition

So, there is a chance for promotion. You want it. You want that next step up. This promotion fits in with your long-term plan. This is the ideal time and opportunity for you to make that step. Trouble is you aren't alone in the running. There are other people to take into account—and eliminate of course. Obviously, for any appointment there are two categories of candidates:

* The internal candidate
* The external candidate

The internal ones are your immediate colleagues, staff from other departments, staff from other branches, staff from other disciplines. If it's your immediate colleagues, chances are you know full well who is interested and who isn't. Staff from other departments should be identified by checking your sources—you should have the ear of every favourite in every department (*see Rule 89*). Staff from other branches present a bit of a challenge but you should use your contacts for such information (*Rule 48*). Candidates from other disciplines within the same organization are the real test. Often you won't know about them until they suddenly appear at interview stage. When I worked for American Express way back in the early 1970s, I was in line for a promotion to

Department Supervisor. I had eliminated all the potential competition from among my own colleagues, checked out the opposition from other departments and branches—there wasn't any—and felt secure and relaxed when, hey presto, a new candidate appeared from a completely separate but parallel discipline. I was accounts and this person was from security. Security, I ask you, what did they know about accounts supervision? The senior management obviously thought they knew a great deal because they got the job. I hadn't had the chance to undermine them. I was taken unawares. Never again.

Candidates from outside the company are very tricky. You have no idea who will apply. But you can:

- See the advert before it goes to press and have a pretty good idea of what is being asked for
- Use contacts to find out who is on the shortlist from outside
- Again use contacts to find out who is being called for interview and what sort of competition you are up against

Remember that knowledge is power. You may not like what you find out, but at least you will know.

Study Them Closely

If you are going for a promotion and there is competition, you need to read, understand, and completely grasp what is being asked for. You need to tailor your resumé, application document, and interview technique, so that you fully fit the picture of the ideal candidate. And you have to study what the competition is doing. Suppose the job is for a supervisory departmental head of the computer sales division. You know that you have:

- Experience of sales
- Experience of computers
- But little experience of supervising other staff

Now check out the opposition. Suppose there are two other candidates:

- Tony has a good working knowledge of the products, good supervisory experience, but knows absolutely nothing about sales.
- Sandra is good on the sales side, has excellent supervisory experience, but doesn't understand the product at all.

Who is the ideal candidate? It depends entirely on what the management is looking for—or what they think they are looking for. The job obviously needs three parts—sales, product knowledge, and supervisory duties. You have two out of three—as do the other two candidates. But which one is the most important to the management? You need to check this out carefully:

- Read the job description.
- Liase with whoever is doing the job now.
- Research what the management is thinking.

If the focus is on one of the two areas you are strong in, then you have already eliminated one of the candidates. Now it's a two-horse race. If, however, the third option is the focus—supervision—the one area you are weak in, then you will have to swing the focus more toward your own skills and experience. At interview you will have to find good reasons why your lack of experience doesn't discount you—talk up the product and how essential it is to have a good knowledge of it and its potential, talk up the importance of sales and how the department lives or dies by its sales record

Obviously this is just an example, the real world is much more complicated.

Don't Backstab

The one thing you won't do in your race to the top is backstab. You will not take out the opposition by unlawful means. It is OK to talk up your own talents and skills and to cleverly influence what management is looking for by highlighting your own expertise and the *implied* failings of your competition. You can imply, suggest, and insinuate. What you cannot do is state openly and honestly why you think they are useless. You make out that they are not up to the promotion by getting the management to focus on how good you are, not by pointing out how bad they are.

The things you do not do are:

- Bad mouth the opposition
- Backstab the competition
- Speak ill of anyone (*see Part 4*)
- Tell lies about the other contestants (*see Rule 44*)
- Reveal secret information about the competition that you have found out that could affect their chances
- Steal information
- Peek, pry, or spy

These are what you must not do. But what can you do then? Well, you can:

- Use any contacts you have to find out the quality of the competition.

- Enhance your own attributes creatively based on what the management is looking for.
- Talk up your own good points, highlighting special skills and expertise you have that they are lacking—you don't say they haven't got what it takes, you make sure the management knows that you do.
- Sell management something they may not have even known they wanted, which the opposition hasn't got.

> "YOU WILL NOT TAKE OUT THE OPPOSITION BY UNLAWFUL MEANS."

RULE 94

Know the Psychology of Promotion

Suppose a vacancy has arisen internally. You really want that job. It fits in with your game plan. You could do with the extra money. You have the expertise, the experience, and the qualifications. You think you will apply for the post. All well and good. But what is being decided here? And what are the criteria being used?

You think job X is vacant, therefore, person Y will fill the post just so long as they have the right attributes. But what are the right attributes? Oh, I know you'll say:

- Experience
- Qualifications
- Expertise

Just like you've got and that's why you are a perfect candidate. Not quite true I'm afraid. There is usually a whole lot more going on than you know. For instance the post may be being advertised because:

- Head office says it has to be but your management has no intention of filling it:

- Your manager has already unofficially filled it—it's been offered to someone already in secret.

- The job is being downsized, it will go to someone who will be laid off in six months' time.

- The whole exercise is a waste of time—the person already doing the job has resigned but they are going to withdraw that at the last minute, they're just holding out for more money at the moment.

- It's an exercise in getting rid of someone, they'll offer it to someone completely unsuitable, so they have grounds to fire them which they can't do in their current position.

- The job is being created so the manager can give it to their favorite/lover/friend/relative/blackmailer.

I don't want to make you paranoid but there are a million and one reasons why you may not get the job despite being, on paper, the best person for it. There may also be a million reasons why you shouldn't apply. You have to know all this. Study the psychology of whatever is being offered. It may not be quite what it seems. Don't buy any cigars off any wooden Indians.

Don't Give Too Much Away

It is probably advisable not to tell anyone that you:

- Intend applying for a new position within the company
- Intend applying for a new job outside of the company
- Are thinking of leaving anyway
- Are thinking of asking for a pay raise
- Are thinking of changing your working schedules
- Are a Rules Player

Don't blab to anyone of anything you are doing. It might be seen as bragging—a Rules Player never brags about anything, we are quiet humility itself—or it might give rise to gossip and we know the rule about that, don't we. And the truth is that even if you only tell one person things leak out. They tell their closest friend and they tell theirs. And so on it goes until you are being hauled before the boss and interrogated as to why you are leaving next Monday when all you had done was say you were thinking about it to Susan in the lunchroom. If you do reveal stuff about yourself you are liable to:

- Chinese whispers (is it PC to still call it that, and if not, what do we call it now?)
- Rumor, gossip, and an opportunity for others to possibly use it against you

> ## "DON'T EVEN ALLOW YOURSELF THE PRIVILEGE OF THINKING OUT LOUD. KEEP YOUR OWN COUNSEL AND YOU WON'T GO WRONG."

- Give the opposition an unfair advantage
- Give the management information they shouldn't be privy to at this stage

Don't even allow yourself the privilege of thinking out loud. Keep your own counsel and you won't go wrong. What you intend doing is entirely up to you. If you need information and anyone asks you why you need it, invent something entirely bogus. No, this is not lying, it is throwing them off the scent. Don't lie, but you can be circumspect, devious, inventive, creative, eccentric, and you are allowed to set up a decoy.

If someone asks you directly if you are thinking about applying for a particular position you can always brush it off, "Oh, always thinking about applying." Does this mean yes or no? Remember don't lie, don't say, "No," when it is plainly untrue and will be seen to be such when you do apply.

RULE 96

Keep Your Ear to the Ground

If you don't know what is going on, how can you make informed decisions or coordinate your career plan. It might be as simple as someone applying for a position you had in mind. If they are more experienced, better qualified, have more expertise and skill in that area then you might be sensible holding back. If you don't you will probably fail—and a Rules Player is always successful.

Now you don't want gossip, you want hard facts. You want to know what is going on without having to listen to tittle-tattle and idle chit-chat. Therefore, it makes sense to:

- Use your contacts for information from other departments.
- Pay attention at meetings. It is often surprising how much information you can pick up by reading between the lines.
- Watch and listen for the "hidden agendas," what people are saying might mask what is really going on.
- Cultivate the office favorite/s and you'll find that they invariably know stuff mere mortals aren't privy to—you'll just have to get them to spill the beans.
- Keep abreast of things like the trade press as you may pick up bits of information that have been 'leaked' to the press before the rank and file have been told—that new merger,

the takeover, the acquisition of a rival company, all these can be useful snippets of information that can put you one step ahead of colleagues and competitors.

A lot of people don't get anywhere *with* their job because they spend far too much time *doing* their job. You need to get your head up from time to time and look around you. You might find the herd has moved on while you were busy feeding and now you are alone and forgotten.

> "A LOT OF PEOPLE DON'T GET ANYWHERE *WITH* THEIR JOB BECAUSE THEY SPEND FAR TOO MUCH TIME *DOING* THEIR JOB."

Make the Opposition Seem Irreplaceable

We have looked at why you can't indulge in any backstabbing—*Rule 93: Don't Backstab*—and you know you can't say anything bad about anyone—*Part 4: If You Can't Say Anything Nice—Shut Up*—but all the same, one of the competition is getting in a bit too close with the boss and it looks like that promotion might just go their way. What do you do? You make them seem irreplaceable of course. But you do it by pointing out all the important but mundane jobs they do. You point out their strengths to your boss in the boring, humdrum areas. "God, I don't know what we'd do without Rachael to do the filing. She must be a Virgo, she's so good at that sort of stuff." But you are only going to point out things that your rival is genuinely good at. We are not going to lie—*Rule 44: Never Lie*—but merely praise the competition for a particular skill. And a skill that they can best exercise right where they are.

Your boss is your customer—you sell your services to them. Your colleagues are the competition. If you were selling cars and someone asked if the next car dealership sold better cars, what would you say? You wouldn't say, "Yes, they sell much better cars than us—and cheaper, in fact you ought to go

> # "YOUR BOSS IS
> # YOUR CUSTOMER.
> # YOUR COLLEAGUES
> # ARE THE
> # COMPETITION."

straight there and buy one of theirs right now." But you also wouldn't say anything bad—"Their cars are all stolen"—but you might well say, "Their cars are fine but they appeal to a different customer, they sell more family sedans than us." You haven't lied. You have indirectly flattered your customer—the implication being, "You obviously need a much more upmarket executive car than those shoddy little boxes they sell next door"—but you haven't said anything bad.

You can also get your rival colleague to ask questions of themselves about the new position: "If you did get Richard's job how do you think you'd cope with all those meetings? I remember you telling me you hated meetings." Hopefully she'll think about all those dreary interminable, intimidating meetings and may well back off. You, on the other hand, find them stimulating, exciting, and very productive—and you haven't said anything bad, merely asked a simple question. You'll get them to want to stay right where they are—they'll make *themselves* irreplaceable.

Don't Damn the Opposition with Faint Praise

The last rule may have seemed as if we were approaching something underhand or devious or ruthless. It isn't. Everything has to be meant, genuine, and honest. Don't praise them. Not unless you really mean it. It is so easy to undermine someone by using praise when you are actually being rather horrible and sabotaging them. You may think this a clever approach. It isn't. You will be seen through immediately and come across as shallow, vindictive, and really rather ruthless. Remember *Part 4: If You Can't Say Anything Nice—Shut Up*? Well, you may think that you can get away with saying nasty things disguised as nice things but you can't. This is the sort of thing that is forbidden:

- "Oh, I know Bill is brilliantly wacky, he is such an independent thinker, he really does operate outside of the box, he's so original and off the wall."

What you're really saying: he's a lone wolf who is slightly nuts and shouldn't be trusted supervising a chimps' tea party let alone an entire department:

- "Bill is such a determined worker. He doesn't care how much it costs, he goes for the last detail of a job. Superb resolution. He likes to see things through to the very end, no matter what. I admire his ability to just not see the dollar signs on a project and instead focus on the application."

What you're really saying: he should never be trusted with his own money, let alone someone else's:

- "Bill really is one of the guys. He really knows how to let his hair down and have fun. I admire his ability to hold his liquor. If there's a wacky stunt going on Bill is always in on it, he is such a free spirit and so youth orientated."

What you're really saying: He's a drunk, a bit wild, not to be trusted looking after staff, and he has the mental age of a teenager:

- "We can't keep Bill in the office. He's such a live wire. I don't think our little cage is big enough for someone with that much energy. I envy him. I sit here doing the paperwork while he's off, out there talking to customers and liasing and being brilliant at sales."

What you're really saying: Bill is crap at paperwork. Don't get into this trap. Your seniors will see through it and if they are decent people they aren't going to like it.

Capitalize on the Career-Enhancing Moments

Every now and then there is a break from the routine, the humdrum, the everyday. These moments of intense activity or public limelight are your moments to enhance your career. They can be:

* The initial selection interview
* Your first day
* Running a presentation
* Running an exhibition
* Chairing an important meeting
* Being put in charge of staff training
* Handling a crisis
* Negotiating with the unions
* Attending a Health and Safety committee meeting
* Being a first aider
* Organizing the staff function

- Being responsible for the visit of a dignitary or celebrity
- Editing the newsletter
- Dealing with the media
- Supervising the office relocation

A lot of people, when first presented with such an option, will be filled with dismay and horror. "Oh, not," they cry, "Not running the exhibition stand at the tradeshow this year. Why me? Oh Lord, why me?"

You, on the other hand, know this rule—this is a career-enhancing moment and you had better take the opportunity to shine. There are no bad jobs, only bad attitude to jobs.

Always look for ways of making such jobs better, more interesting, slicker, quicker, and realize that they are providing you with the wherewithal to shine.

> "THERE ARE NO BAD JOBS, ONLY BAD ATTITUDE TO JOBS."

RULE 100

Cultivate the Friendship and Approval of Your Colleagues

If you follow all the rules outlined in this book you will be a thoroughly nice person, likeable, confident, agreeable, and assured. You will be grown up but still a lot of fun to be around. You need the support of your fellow co-workers to advance and you need their friendship and approval. If you don't have these things, you open yourself up to the possibility of being sabotaged, pulled down, dumped upon, or fired. But how do you cultivate their friendship and approval when you are doing everything to get promoted above them, to be their boss?

What you have to do is be one of the guys/gals while retaining a modicum of detachment. You have to run with the sheep and hunt with the wolves. You have to be "one of them" *and* one of the bosses.

You'll need to socialize with the staff without losing control, getting drunk, sleeping with any of them, or getting involved. Laugh at their jokes, but don't go on vacation with them. Listen to their troubles but don't tell them they are trivial or inconsequential. Support them and nurture them when they are under pressure but remain calm at all times yourself. You have to become their mother hen at the same time as their friend and fellow conspirator. You have to listen to their complaints and moans about management and the boss without revealing who you really are—their eventual new boss.

You have to help them with their work so they get to rely on you. You have to be the diplomat, the conciliator, the referee, the pal, and the priest. You have to get them to love you because you are so nice, so friendly yourself.

You have to be their tower of strength and their prop and their chum. You have to make them feel special, feel that without you their lives are gray and dull and boring. You have to be the life and soul of the party and the party organizer and the one who clears up afterward.

All this is possible, not easy but possible. If you get on the right side of your colleagues to such an extent, it will be them who push you forward, them that want you to be their boss, demand of you that you lead. You will be the Rules Player *par excellence.*

Notes

Notes

The Rules of Management
A Definitive Code for Managerial Success
BY RICHARD TEMPLAR

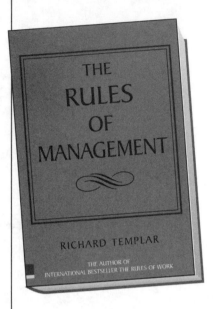

You're smart, talented, competent, responsible.
So...they made you a manager.
And suddenly, all that good stuff...just ain't enough.

You need to know what the greatest managers know:
The Rules of Management.
Here they are. All 100 of 'em.
For managing teams. For managing you.

Read 'em. Learn 'em. Live 'em.
Next thing you know, you'll be looking good.
Relaxed. Confident. Assertive.
In charge. In control.

You'll be building, leading teams that
do the impossible, follow you anywhere, and
bring passion to work
(yes, even at your company).

The Rules of Management: they're not just rules.
They're your blueprint for greatness,
and shortcut to the executive suite.

ISBN 013187036X, © 2006, 240 pp., $16.95

Winning Habits
4 Secrets That Will Change the Rest of Your Life
BY DICK LYLES

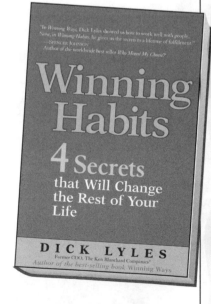

"In WINNING HABITS, Dick gives us the secrets of a lifetime of fulfillment."

—Spencer Johnson, Author of the worldwide best seller *Who Moved My Cheese?*

WINNING HABITS is a powerful parable that identifies the four fundamental habits at the heart of success in business and in life—and shows exactly how readers can apply those habits in their own lives. The 4 secrets that will change the rest of readers' lives are: 1) Be first on, last off, and add extra value; 2) Never trade results for excuses; 3) Solve problems in advance; 4) Always make those around you look good.

ISBN 0131453580, © 2004, 128 pp., $19.95